Making Word Work for You

An Editor's Intro to the Tool of the Trade

Hilary Powers

EDITORIAL
FREELANCERS
ASSOCIATION

Editorial Freelancers Association
71 West 23rd Street, 4th Floor
New York, NY 10010
www.the-efa.org

Editor: Elaine Will Sparber
Designer and compositor: Helen Glenn Court
Indexer: Shoshana Hurwitz
Cover designer: Mary Ratcliffe

EFA is a national nonprofit volunteer organization of professionals who provide freelance editorial services to the publishing and communications industries. EFA members live all over the United States and abroad, and are experienced in a wide range of professional skills, subject areas, and media. Members include abstractors, copyeditors, designers, desktop publishing experts, editors, indexers, manuscript evaluators, picture researchers, project managers, proofreaders, researchers, textbook development editors, translators, and writers.

While every precaution has been taken in the preparation of this book, the publisher and the author assume no responsibility for errors or omissions, or for damages resulting from the use of the information contained herein.

Making Word Work for You is an independent publication and is not affiliated with, nor has it been authorized, sponsored, or otherwise approved by Microsoft Corporation.

Microsoft, Internet Explorer, and Outlook are either registered trademarks or trademarks of Microsoft Corporation in the United States and other countries.

All other trademarks are the property of their respective owners.

Library of Congress Cataloging-in-Publication Data

Powers, Hilary.
   Making Word work for you : an editor's intro to the tool of the trade / Hilary Powers.
      p. cm.
   Summary: "A guide for professional editors to using Microsoft Word to edit manuscripts"—
   Provided by publisher.
   Includes index.
   ISBN-13: 978-1-880407-22-6 (trade pbk.)
   ISBN-10: 1-880407-22-1 (trade pbk.)
 1. Microsoft Word. 2. Editing. I. Title.
   Z52.5.M52P69 2007
   005.52—dc22
                                                    2007033142

Printed in the United States of America.

CONTENTS

Author's Note

I didn't plan to update this book until I could talk about Word beyond 2003, but one section of the original—the long whinge about how much I miss voice command processing—became obsolete. I found out that all the voice software I needed was at my fingertips at the time I wrote that, and you have it too if you have Word 2002 or later. While I was explaining how to use that feature, I went ahead and added the twenty or so new tips and tricks, or refinements of old ones, that had accumulated since my last chance to work on this.

LATE NEWS! August 20, 2009: I just learned that the next release of Word will have a customizable ribbon. Now I'm looking forward to upgrading instead of dreading it.

Introduction: With Your Computer, Not Just on It

Assuming you already know how to edit, you can edit in Word. Well, you can edit in Word if you know how to get at the files and make changes in them—beyond file open, type in, delete, and save, the absolute skill requirement is essentially zero. But you won't like the experience much. You'll probably soon join the ranks of those who maintain that editing in Word is harder than editing on paper, more exposed to error and less conducive to physical health, and generally a bad deal all around.

The problem isn't in the tool, though. It is in its use. If you really want your computer to act like a stack of paper and a set of colored pencils, you can make it do so. Sort of. But if instead you use it for what it is—which requires a different approach to the work and a different set of tricks from those that make for effective paper editing—editing in Word becomes easier (and faster) than editing on paper, and neither less accurate nor harder on your body.

The biggest difference between paper editing and onscreen editing is that a straight line is no longer the shortest distance between two points. That is, the steps in the edit are different, and there are more of them, and tasks may happen in a different order from what would work best on paper, but the final effect is that high-quality, medium-level commercial editing—giving a publisher two full read-throughs with substantive overtones and addressing thoughtful queries to the author—can be done at a net rate (considering all the pages and all the time spent on the job) that should come in anywhere between half again faster and triple what you can do on paper.

Hard to swallow? Read on. . . .

Where We're Going

A full description of Microsoft Word and all its uses in all sorts of editing could easily run ten times the size of this little book, so I've had to make a lot of choices about what to present and how to present it. The reader I pictured when deciding whose interests should govern the selection is someone who has fairly substantial experience as a copyeditor of books or journal articles and just enough knowledge of Word to get a file open and start trying to work by instinct. If all goes well, that reader will find enough solid information about Word here (and more to the point, enough of the mind-set of Word-whacking) to make the program feel like a cooperative and friendly tool instead of an interfering and alien environment.

If your experience or interests differ, please bear with me. There's still a lot for you here, but you might want to pick and choose based on this introduction and the subheads in the table of contents, or look things up in the index, rather than reading straight through.

Those who do read from cover to cover will start by getting acquainted with what Word can do without worrying about the details of how to do it. After all, there's a lot to keep track of about this everything-for-everybody all-purpose tool, and the first and most important thing to know is why you might want to know any of the rest of it.

Then the book follows Word from its plain-vanilla state—what you get when you load the CD and open the program for the first time—through more and more active ways to make it stop doing its thing and start doing yours. *Note:* Almost everything here addresses ways to modify text rather than ways to make a manuscript look like a finished book. That reflects the state of my knowledge: I know lots about text manipulation and almost nothing about formatting, because in my corner of the editing world, the essential info about formatting mostly involves ways to get rid of it.

Here's a brief outline:

- *Chapter 1. The Shortest Distance: A Concrete Example:* A detour to the world of travel for a detailed example of the way the mind-set of *using* Word differs from that of making paper procedures work onscreen. This mind-set is what allows me to claim such astonishing speed boosts for real electronic editing.
- *Chapter 2. Building a Working Environment:* What you see on the basic Word 2003 screen (or could see with a few mouse clicks), and what to do if you don't like it.
- *Chapter 3. Finding Work for Word's Idle Hands:* Where Word hides the settings that make it second-guess what you're doing, how to fix them, and how to use the basic services the program offers, including AutoCorrect, Find and Replace, and the spelling checker.
- *Chapter 4. Deploying the Custom Features:* Where to get hold of the things Word is built to do but won't volunteer, like keeping track of vocabulary you don't want to use even though it's properly spelled, rearranging the keyboard, and running your own commands.
- *Chapter 5. Domesticating Tracked Changes:* How to use the built-in tracking feature smoothly and comfortably, and how to keep its markup simple enough to avoid frightening your authors.

- *Chapter 6. Coping with Snares and Pitfalls:* Where Word's bodies are buried, and how to keep them from rising from their graves and haunting your work.
- *Chapter 7. Locating Useful Additions:* Sources of tools, books, and ongoing advice about Word.
- *Chapter 8. A Bouquet of Sample Shortcuts:* Some easy—and easily understood—macros to start your collection and give you some resources to cannibalize for your first adventures in your own command development.
- *Chapter 9. Walking Through a Job:* The steps involved in a fairly generic nonfiction edit, with notes on ways I use Word to help in the process.

The rest of this introduction discusses the differences among various Word versions and outlines the terminology used in the book.

WHAT WORD TO USE

The main PC Word versions in play now are 97, 2000, 2002, 2003, and 2007, and for the moment the keepers are 2000 and 2003. Word 97 is somewhat unstable, and Word 2002 is hardly better than beta software; 2003 is the play-tested version, with most of the errors and many of the idiocies rendered harmless. If you're happy with 2000, there's little need to upgrade; it's reasonably stable, and it'll do just about anything you might need as an editor. Word 2003 is even more resistant to trouble, however, and includes some moderately useful stuff that you might find worthwhile. If you're using 2002, you should definitely upgrade to 2003. It's getting harder to find as the years pass, but as of mid-2009, you can still buy the software from a reliable source on the Internet for less than $250 if you shop around, and it'll make a big difference to your comfort level.

Why not upgrade past 2003? I recommend waiting for clients to take that leap first. For one thing, the default file format has changed, and it'll take a while for viewers and readers to catch up. In addition, Word 2007 has— what joy—a completely different interface, sans menus, with no plan to make the old display available. (Before this book went to press, a company called Addintools [www.addintools.com] released Classic Menu for Office 2007, an inexpensive product that provides something like the old menus in the new environment. *Office Watch*, a well-respected electronic newsletter, says that Classic Menu works well and with no adverse effects its people could see—so there's hope if you upgrade and decide you hate the new interface.)

Word 2007 is not a disaster; most macros and add-ins continue to work properly in the new environment, and the new user interface has much to recommend it. Me, I'll probably upgrade eventually—but I'll give the new design a bit longer to settle down first. I went straight from Word 97 to 2003, and never regretted missing the intervening versions.

On the Mac side, the versions to hang on to are Word 98 if you're using OS 9 and Word X if you're using OS X. Word 2004 maps to Word 2002, not 2003 as you might think, and it shares the disadvantages of its parent. Word 2003 was never ported to the Mac; Microsoft skipped straight to Word 2008, which is Word 2007 minus the VBA macro language. That left Mac users who upgraded past Word 2004 trying to figure out ways to get equivalent macros working in AppleScript. Many turned to figuring out how to apply pressure to Microsoft instead, and the latest news is that the next version of Word for the Mac will once again support VBA.

Note: If you're on a PC with Word 2003, the things I talk about in this book should work for you just as described. With anything back to Word 97, most of it will work, but some of the file locations will be different and some things won't appear at all. If you're on a Mac, a lot of it—including almost all the basic concepts, for the 2004 edition, anyway—will work, but screen locations as well as file locations may differ, and commands may be more different than just substituting Command for Ctrl and Option for Alt. The dialogs found on a PC at Tools, Options are at Tools, Preferences in Word 98 and at Word, Preferences in Word X and later on a Mac.

Finding a Common Language

You don't need a lot of jargon to keep up with explanations of things to do with Word. Nonetheless, some terms wind up with meanings you won't see elsewhere, and it's useful to get those down first.

Things

- *Insertion point:* The place on the screen where the next typed character will appear when you *press* a key; usually shown by a blinking vertical line.
- *Mouse pointer:* The symbol that indicates where the pointing device (mouse, trackball, touchpad, whatever; they all use a *mouse pointer*) is focused; it doesn't blink, and its shape indicates what will happen if you *click* it: usually, move the *insertion point* or activate a *menu*, a *toolbar* icon, or a virtual *button*.

- *Key:* One of the thingies on the keyboard; it makes something happen when you *press* it.
- *Button:* (Physical) One of the thingies on the pointing device; it makes something happen when you push on it. (Virtual) An area on the screen that is colored to resemble a physical *button*; it makes something happen when you *click* it with the pointing device.
- *Menu:* A list of sets of actions Word will do for you: File, Edit, View, and so on.
- *Submenu:* A set of items that reveals itself when you *click* something on a *menu.* In this book, I indicate cascading sequences of submenus by separating the titles with commas—for example, "Insert, Reference, Footnote" gets you to the dialog where you can insert or reformat footnotes and endnotes.
- *Toolbar:* A collection of virtual buttons (also called *icons*), each of which performs a specific action when you *click* it.
- *Pilcrow:* A paragraph mark—the character Word uses on screen to indicate what's still—from typewriter days—called a *hard carriage return.* It looks like this: ¶.
- *Cursor:* Obsolete term for *insertion point,* dating from the pre-mouse era. It's still sometimes used interchangeably for *insertion point* or *mouse pointer,* making it more or less useless; I mention it only because you may be wondering when I'm going to get to it.

Actions

- *Press:* Activate a *key* on the keyboard, producing a character on the screen or causing some programmed action to take place.
- *Click:* Move the *mouse pointer* to whatever is named and do whatever the pointing device requires to activate it for the indicated purpose—push on a physical *button,* tap on a touchpad, whatever.
- *Double-click:* Move the *mouse pointer* to whatever is named and do whatever the pointing device requires to activate it for the indicated purpose—push on one physical *button* twice, push once on a different physical *button,* tap a touchpad quickly twice, whatever.
- *Right-click:* Move the *mouse pointer* to whatever is named and do whatever the pointing device requires to activate the pop-up menu of chores you can tell the computer to do at that spot on the screen. The name comes from your basic mouse set up for right-handed use, where you get the effect by pushing on the right-most physical *button.*

- *Select:* Highlight something on the screen so that you can copy, delete, or otherwise manipulate it.

Key Patterns

- *Individual key:* Indicated by whatever is printed on the face: "Press the A key" means to press that key with no modifiers (as if you were typing the lowercase letter *a*).
- *Simultaneous combinations:* "Press Shift+A" means you should press both keys at the same time; in this case you would type the uppercase letter *A*. Other combinations involve Ctrl (usually Command on a Mac, though Macs also make some use of the Ctrl key), Alt (Option on a Mac), or any two or three of these modifiers. ("Press Ctrl+Shift+F9" calls for pressing all three keys together.)
- *Sequential combinations:* "Press Alt+A, C" means you should press Alt and A (that is, lowercase *a*) together, release them, and then press C.

Getting Started

OK. Enough noodling. Time to sit down at the screen and start to play. . . .

Play is the operative word, by the by; I can tell you a lot about the kinds of things Word does, but I can't begin to cover the details. In any case, to make the best use of Word, you need to fiddle with it for yourself—futz with the various menus and see what the different settings do on your machine.

So when I stop and recommend that you work through a menu on your own or read another source, that's not a cop-out. It's an introduction to a basic insight about using a computer:

Don't get mad, get even.

That is, if you don't like what the beast does, fiddle with it until you do—nine times in ten, you have a cure for the problem at your fingertips, but no one else can read your mind and tell you everything you need.

1 The Shortest Distance: A Concrete Example

Forget editing for a moment. Suppose you want to go from New York to San Francisco. . . .

The most straightforward approach is to don a good pair of boots and start walking: go out the door and take the shortest combination of streets and roads that will get you there, cutting cross-country when you can. But it'd be a lot quicker to make plane reservations, call a cab, ride thirty miles in the wrong direction, dillyfrog around the airport for a couple of hours getting through security, and hike onto a commercial jet before you start moving in the direction you really want to go.

A plane shortens your travel time by getting above the obstacles and diversions of foot slogging, and by going very, very fast. A computer shortens your edit time by implementing your choices very, very quickly and tirelessly; it doesn't get bored going over the same stuff time and again, and it doesn't get irritated or make a mess if you change your mind.

So suppose you're working on a trade book in the social sciences whose authors have bolstered their observations with citations to a couple of hundred other published works. Your job—and it doesn't matter what tools you're using—is to confirm that every source in the reference section is cited somewhere in the text, every citation in the text leads to one source in the reference section, all the formatting is sound, and all the names and dates are consistent.

You can just edit the citations along with everything else—that is, pause whenever you get to one, tick it off on a copy of the reference list, and make whatever adjustments or queries it calls for. *Let's see, here's Williams on page 25 of the ref list ... here's Jensen—oops, Jenson—on page 10; gotta query that ... here's Morris on page 13 ... and here's Williams—is it the same Williams?—back on 25. ...* But it's not that bad; in fact, it probably takes no more than a minute per citation, and they often tend to cluster in parts of a document and leave other parts more or less without distractions.

But there are bunches and lots of them. Two hundred sources, cited an average of five times apiece in the manuscript; that's pushing a thousand minutes. More than fifteen hours. And that doesn't consider the time it will cost you to deal with the thirty-five or forty referenced sources that (probably) didn't get cited after all in the final draft, or the eighty-nine citations to sources that never got included or are so screwed up you can't be sure. Meanwhile, it's dangerous to skip checking a citation just because it looks familiar. Nine times out of ten, you may be right in figuring it's OK, but the tenth is going to have a misspelled name or erroneous date, and if you don't catch it, someone else probably will—and will wonder what sort of doofus did the edit.

(Yes, of course, I'm pulling numbers out of the air here, and with an axe to grind besides. You can probably do it faster. But the bedrock truth remains: checking citations against references with everything on paper is a tedious and grueling chore.)

So what can the computer do for you here? If you treat the citations as a separate work unit, the computer can cut the overall time required to vet them all to a tiny fraction of what the paper process takes. The main savings comes from eliminating paper-shuffling; when you deal with all the citations to a source at once, you never have to go back to it. You also save time by automating much of the query process.

The steps involved are all dead easy, all computer-assisted, and many of them can be done in bulk rather than by fiddling with the citations one by one. For now, that's all you need to know about how they work. (You'll find explanations for all of them in later chapters.)

Here's an overview of what you do:

1. *Make your plane reservations.* Jump from citation to citation, ignoring everything else.
    a. In each citation, fix any formatting errors you happen to notice. (It doesn't matter much if you miss something, but fixes now will be faster than fixes later.) If you see reliable patterns of error—say, the author uses *et al.* and the client wants *and others*—close the documents you're working on and fix the errors for all the manuscript files at once.
    b. Make a copy of each citation (or group of citations) and paste it into another file.
2. *Call a taxicab.* After you pull the citation copies for a whole chapter, make sure every citation is on a line of its own. Then label them all with their chapter number at the end of the line.
3. *Go to the airport and make your way through security.* Once you have all the citations for the book copied, get them ready to check.
    a. Sort them by first author.

b. Look over the list; if any author has too many titles and coauthors to identify all the works easily at a glance, do a further sort of that group by coauthor, by date, or both.

c. Lay out the citation copies single-spaced and in two columns to get as many onto a page as feasible while still being easy to read.

d. Print them out on scratch paper.

4. *Get on the plane and fly.* Check the citations.

a. Open the reference file.

b. Put the printout in a comfortable spot near the screen, and vet each citation as you come to it on the list.

   (1) If it matches an entry in the reference file: Check it off on the printout.

   (2) If several citations match the same source: Make sure they really are identical, then draw one line through them to clear them as a group.

   (3) If a citation (or group of citations) has no matching reference: Open the indicated chapter or chapters and put a standard query at each citation.

   (4) If a reference has no citation: Have your computer check through the files to see if the author is mentioned anywhere. If you get any hits, open the indicated files and check to see if the source itself is mentioned in a nonstandard way that step 1 missed. If it's really not cited, put a standard query in the reference section, asking for citation or removal of the source.

   (5) If names or dates differ: Put more-or-less standard queries on both the citation and the reference entry.

   (6) If a citation has formatting errors: Open the indicated chapter file and fix them.

The details make these steps sound more complex than just hiking cross-country, I know—but the detour really does make just as much difference to the amount of sweat involved in the journey. And this little book includes all the techniques you need to make it work—for pointers, just watch for the 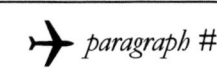 airplane notes like the one shown, which will refer you to the appropriate numbered paragraph here.

2 BUILDING A WORKING ENVIRONMENT

Well, you already *have* a working environment. The first trick is to find out what Word will do for you right now, with nothing added. Figure 1 gives you a quick look at your new friend.

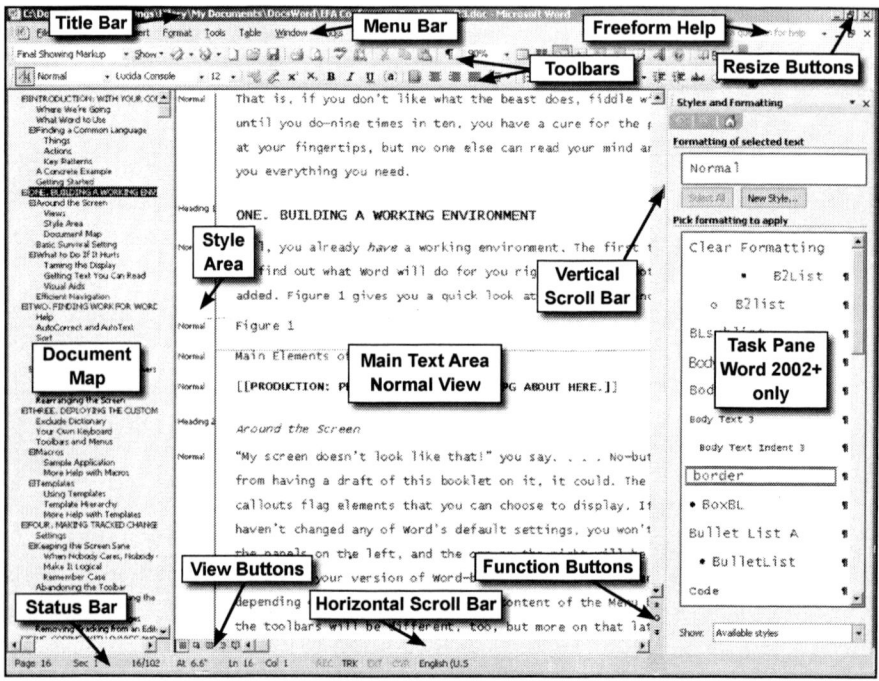

Figure 1. Main Elements of the Word 2003 Screen

AROUND THE SCREEN

"My screen doesn't look like that!" you say. ... No—but aside from having a draft of this book on it, it could. The callouts flag elements that you can choose to display. If you haven't changed any of Word's default settings, you won't see the panels on the left, and the one on the right will be there if it's in your version of Word—but the content will change depending on what you're doing. The content of the menu bar and the toolbars will be different, too, but more on that later. The following sections give you detail on some of this stuff but don't describe everything labeled in the figure; I've flagged several items just to make sure I can talk about them later.

Views

The view buttons (and the View menu, which is on the menu bar but out of sight behind one of the callouts in the figure) let you change the appearance of the main text area. Figure 1 shows it in Normal view, which is where I spend most of my time, but you can also see whole pages complete with margins (Print Layout view), content as it would appear on the Web (you got it, Web Layout view), two pages side by side like a paperback book (Reading Layout view; needs a recent version of Word), and an Outline view that lets you collapse and expand sections of the document and move stuff around without looking at it, which I've always found too scary to mess with. If you need to work in Print Layout view and you have Word 2002+, you can conserve screen real estate by mousing over the space between the pages. When the mouse pointer changes to a pair of little boxes with arrows, click to hide the white space at the top and bottom of each page. Mouse over and click again to get the margins (and headers and footers) back in sight.

There's also a Print Preview that shows you exactly what Word thinks your printer will do with the file, but it's not here—get it at File, Print Preview. Its biggest use is to check for bleeds and the lineup of two-page spreads.

As I said, I prefer Normal view, switching to Print Layout view only to look for things that Normal hides: text boxes and other graphic elements. With files fresh from the client, it's useful to switch to Print Layout view at least once early on, then drop the zoom factor (on the Standard toolbar) down to 20 percent or so. You won't be able to read anything, but graphic elements will stand out like mold on cheese—especially if you pick up on the advice later in this chapter and change the white background to a color that provides less glare.

Style Area

When you're in Normal view, this charming column (opened at Tools, Options, View, Style area width) tells you what style is assigned to each paragraph in the document. Keep it closed if you don't care about styles, but it's well worth half or three-quarters of an inch of screen real estate if the styles matter—especially if your client expects you to fix the styles as well as the text. In fact, if you have to play with styles, it's priceless; double-click on a name there to open the Style dialog, where you can add, delete, and modify the little beasts.

Document Map

The Document Map (on/off toggle on the View menu and the matching icon on the Standard toolbar, and by voice command if you've set up Speech) gives you what amounts to a hot-linked table of contents for the whole file, visible on screen whenever you want it. Click on a heading on the map pane, and the insertion point and main display move to the same heading in the text of the file. You can also expand and collapse sections to see whatever level of detail is most useful—either individually, using the little plus and minus boxes, or for the list as a whole, by right-clicking at the top or bottom and then choosing the level of display you want to see.

Warning: The Document Map has its little ways. It works best if you use Word's built-in heading styles, and it occasionally gets too enthusiastic. One of the shortcuts in Chapter 8 restores it to a sense of its duty if that happens.

BASIC SURVIVAL SETTINGS

Chapter 3 goes into a lot of detail on setting up Word to behave the way you want it to, but one trick is worth applying right now. Part of the problem with wild Word is that it hides stuff (in the name of efficiency) that you need if you're going to work efficiently.

Go to Tools, Customize, Options and make sure the following boxes are checked:

- Show Standard and Formatting toolbars on two rows
- Always show full menus
- Show ScreenTips on toolbars
- Show shortcut keys in ScreenTips

The rest of that dialog box is harmless. I keep the large icons turned off and the font-names-in-font setting turned on, but neither one makes much difference. However, the defaults that cram the Standard and Formatting toolbars onto one line and strip menus back to the commands you've used recently instead of showing you everything available every time you look are among the silliest things Word does if left to itself. Once you hit your stride in Word, most of the stuff you want all the time will be on your keyboard, and you'll look at the toolbars and menus mainly for unusual things. So what you really want there is what you *haven't* been using; you don't care about what you've used lately.

WHAT TO DO IF IT HURTS

Many people find that looking at the Word screen long enough to get anything done is outright painful, or at least so irritating that it's hard to see errors in the text. And the appearance of the text on the screen—especially the near-invisible punctuation marks—often cuts into editing accuracy. When this happens, the natural inclination is to retreat to paper and print the job out so you can work without suffering, but it's better to change the display instead.

The first thing to try is enlarging the text using View, Zoom. Many people find readability a simple matter of upping the magnification until the type is large enough to feel comfortable. (I don't, so I can't help suspecting that even those who think Zoom is an answer would be better off exploring other options too before deciding on that approach.)

Taming the Display

If you haven't futzed with the settings, the default Word screen is the same as for most other programs controlled by your operating system: white background, black text. Within Word, you have only one alternative: On Tools, Options, General you can check the box that says "Blue background, white text" and get an approximation of the ancient (pre-Windows) working environment. If you don't care for that, either—and you well may not, as the light-letters-on-darkground concept really needs typefaces rather heavier than the modern printemulation fonts—you have to get outside Word to fix it.

In Windows XP, the answer is to go to Control Panel, Display, Appearance, Advanced and reset the colors of all the screen elements to something you like to look at, then save the package as a *theme*. I'm not familiar with other operating systems, but they all should allow you some choice of display.

I like a slate blue working area with dark blue type, because high contrast makes my eyes itch. If your machine will run a Windows XP theme file and you'd like to see what I use, you can download a copy by entering the URL www.powersedit.com/ftp/HScreens.zip on your Web browser's address bar, making sure to get the uppercase and lowercase letters exactly as shown. Unzip the archive to get at the file itself. (Note: This requires an unzip utility program, which you probably already have. If you don't, see "Compression Managers" in Chapter 7, under "Other Support Programs.") No matter where you put the theme file on your hard drive, you should then be able to choose it on the list offered at Control Panel, Display, Themes.

My choice isn't the one true best way for everybody, of course; about half the people who see it like it, and many of the rest run screaming. But if you find your eyes getting tired while you work, the hard black-and-white screen may be the culprit—even if it hasn't occurred to you that it might be a problem. If that's the case, the only way you'll find out is to play with the screen for yourself.

Getting Text You Can Read

Font choice is almost as individual as display environment. The Windows default font, Times New Roman, is dense and reasonably handsome, so most people stay with it, but I find it a disaster for editing. Part of its problem is built-in authority (it looks so much like a printed book, even the errors seem to make sense), and the rest is that it's so dense—and the punctuation marks so small in comparison to the letters—that it's just plain hard to see details. Courier (now Courier New) is the traditional typewriter-style manuscript font, and many publishers use it. My own favorite is Lucida Console, which is denser than Courier New but looks more open, and I do all my work in 12-point Lucida Console zoomed down to 85 percent, switching back to the client's preference before returning a job. In this book, the screen shots that show bits of a file give you a glimpse of Lucida Console, but don't judge it by that—it's a pure screen font and not particularly agreeable on paper. (*Note:* If your work involves non-Roman alphabets or mathematical symbols, check your chosen font for compatibility. Make sure what you see makes sense, and if it doesn't—or you wouldn't know sense from nonsense—look at an unmodified copy of the original file to see if it matches.)

Once again, there's no one best way—but there'll be something you like better than the other choices open to you, and it probably won't be anything a client sends you. With paper, you have to take what you get, but on the screen you can suit yourself.

Warning: Never select a non-Roman font unless you seriously need to use it. If you turn on Arabic or one of the others just to see how it looks, you will trigger Word's alternate language features, many of which make the user interface amazingly more complex. If you've done this and want to get back to normal, go to Start, All Programs, Microsoft Office, Microsoft Office Tools, Microsoft Office 2003 Language Settings and disable everything except the breed of English you're using.

Visual Aids

Still another choice involves what you see on the screen—just the letters and punctuation marks, or what Word refers to as *hidden text*: codes that indicate where the spaces and tabs and some other things are sitting. You can turn the display of hidden text on and off by clicking the pilcrow (¶) on the Standard toolbar, or by pressing Ctrl+Shift+8. Tools, Options, View includes check boxes that let you specify individual codes to show all the time.

I tend to leave hidden text turned off all the time, except when I need to see what's happening at that level.

Efficient Navigation

For real editing speed, the keyboard beats the mouse for almost everything. (After all, which is faster: moving your hand off the keyboard or not moving your hand off the keyboard?) Learn and use the keyboard shortcuts (called *hot keys*) for the things you do most often, and the arrow and movement keys to get around the file. Here are some of the basics:

- *Alt+[Any letter underlined in the name of a menu]:* Open the menu.
- *[Any letter underlined in a word in a menu]:* Activate that feature or expand a submenu or dialog box. *Note:* If you see an ellipsis (a triangle on a Mac) at the right side of the command, you'll get additional choices when you activate it.
- *Arrow keys alone:* Move one character or line in the direction of the arrow per key press.
- *Ctrl+arrow key:* Move one word or paragraph in the direction of the arrow per key press. (If you're in the middle of a paragraph, the up arrow will move to the beginning of that paragraph.)
- *Shift+Arrow key:* Select one character or line in the direction of the arrow per key press.
- *Shift+Ctrl+Arrow key:* Select one word or paragraph in the direction of the arrow per key press. (If you're in the middle of a paragraph, the up and down arrows will select the remainder of that paragraph.)
- *Home or End key alone:* Move to the beginning or end of the line, respectively.
- *Shift+Home/Shift+End:* Select to the beginning or end of the line, respectively.
- *Ctrl+Home/Ctrl+End:* Move to the beginning or end of the file, respectively.
- *Shift+Ctrl+Home/Shift+Ctrl+End:* Select to the beginning or end of the file, respectively.
- *Ctrl+[click]:* Select the sentence where the insertion point is located, plus the following space, if any.
- *Shift+F5:* Go back to the last action; on open, go to the place where the insertion point was located when the file was saved. If you press the combination repeatedly while you're working, it will cycle through the last three places it registered, which will usually turn out to be changes to the text or the results of Find operations.

Note: Shift+F5 is great when it works, but it often doesn't—especially when you want to go someplace, fix a couple of things, and return.

I wound up recording two macros: SetPlace, which puts a bookmark named Place at the current location of the insertion point, and GoPlace, which moves the insertion point to the Place bookmark. On Alt+F5 and Ctrl+F5 respectively, they provide a pretty good go-back function—immune to the troubles that beset Shift+F5, but of course subject to foresight errors; you have to set Place before you need it. (See Chapter 4 for the basics on macros.)

3 Finding Work for Word's Idle Hands

Word has a built-in desire to *do things* for its users. When you don't want what it thinks you should want, it's endlessly annoying—grating on your nerves like a hypercontrolling parent telling you what to wear and what to say. But you can almost always make it stop and remember to stay stopped, and once you get past its "Word Knows Best" approach, what remains is flexible and genuinely helpful.

OPTIONS

How to make it get its nose out of your business? The details would fill a book like this one, but what it boils down to is getting acquainted with all the standard menus. Open a garbage file (any file you don't care about), then start working through the choices. Start with Tools, Customize, Options if you didn't follow the advice under "Basic Survival Settings" in Chapter 2, and then move on to Tools, Options and all the rest. (You'll see a number of specific suggestions about settings throughout this book, but there's no one best way for everyone. If there was, Word would be a lot simpler.) If you don't know what something does, try turning it off and seeing whether Word's behavior changes; you can always turn it back on again if you don't like the results or if you see no apparent change. If you don't see any change and decide to leave something turned off, make a note of what you changed—that way, you have a good start for troubleshooting if something unfortunate shows up later.

HELP

Or check the Help system to find out about mystery options. In Word 2003, Help (accessed via F1, the Help menu, or the free-form question box on the menu bar) is often genuinely helpful; a definite improvement over earlier editions. It's sometimes a challenge to figure out what Word calls whatever it is you want to ask about, but it's worth a try. Before you ask someone else (say, on a discussion list) for aid, put a brief version of the query into the "Type a question for help" box—you may well get a useful answer.

You could also consult the Office Assistant if you haven't already strangled it. If you're seeing it and don't like it, click Help, Hide the Office Assistant. Me, I didn't even install it in my version of Word.

AUTOCORRECT

Tools, AutoCorrect Options (Alt+T, A) opens a dialog with five powerful tabs. The two AutoFormat tabs are where Word hides some of its most annoying compulsive helpfulness; I keep almost everything there turned off, except for curly quotes, built-in heading styles, and tables. The Smart Tags tab invites Word to snuggle up to your text and suggest all sorts of things you might have meant to do instead of what you actually did—none of which I have any use for, so I keep it turned all the way off.

The other two tabs—AutoCorrect and AutoText—both replace what you type with something else specified in their lists. Once you prune the defaults to get rid of things that cause you trouble, like changing "(c)" to the copyright symbol, ©, which is a pain when you're trying to make an in-line list, they are both vastly useful. You can assign text of your own to either AutoCorrect or AutoText by selecting the text, then going to Tools, AutoCorrect Options, clicking the tab for the feature you want, and typing in the trigger characters you plan to use for this text.

AutoCorrect is best for short phrases that need no formatting. (It will do formatted text, but I've found that part of the feature unreliable.) The most efficient way to use it is to check "Replace text as you type" on the tab, but if you do that, be careful to avoid using regular words as triggers for it. For example, if I type "ip," my copy of Word instantly changes it to "Is the preceding sentence OK?" (the query opener I use most often). You wouldn't want to use "is" for that purpose. ... It doesn't tie you up completely, though; if you trigger an AutoCorrect item you don't want, press Ctrl+Z (Undo the last action) immediately and it will go back to what you typed.

AutoText needs a deliberate action to make it take effect. The most efficient way to use it is to check "Show AutoComplete suggestions" on the tab; then, when you type the first four letters of a trigger, you should see a little banner notifying you that you can get the full text if you press Enter from that point on. If you keep typing past the end of the trigger, you get what you type, without the conversion. AutoText entries can be substantially longer than AutoCorrect entries, and they can include all sorts of formatting; for instance, the airplane tip boxes in this book are all based on a master stored in my AutoText collection.

Another difference: You can print a list of AutoText entries straight from Word—go to File, Print, Print What, AutoText entries to send a list to the printer. I used to think it was impossible to print a list of AutoCorrect entries, but Allen Wyatt's Word Tips now has a macro that does the job. Pick it up at http://

word.tips.net/Pages/T000340_Printing_a_List_of_AutoCorrect_Entries.html (http://tinyurl.com/PrintAutoCorrect).

The "standard queries" described in the citation-checking process in Chapter 1 all make use of AutoText entries in a client-specific query shell (see "Templates" in Chapter 4). Here are some of my AutoText triggers and their corresponding stored phrases:

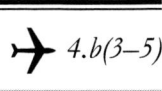 *4.b(3–5)*

- *noref:* "The Reference section lacks an entry for this citation. Please supply."
- *nocite:* "There appears to be no citation to this source in the text. Please either insert one or delete the reference."
- *badname:* "This author's name is spelled differently in text and Reference section. Please fix as needed."
- *baddate:* "The only similar reference has a different date—please adjust as needed."

It's useful to keep AutoCorrect and AutoText entries fairly generic, then go back and edit them as needed. For example, my "badname" text often gets changed—for example, to "*The second author's* name is spelled differently in text and Reference section. Please fix as needed."

Sort

Things happen. Maybe the author stuck things into the bibliography without reading their neighbors carefully enough. The style sheet wants you to put all the special vocabulary in alphabetical order. The elements of a table need resequencing. When you need to put things in a certain order, Word is there to help.

The sorting tool Word gives you is on the Table menu, so you might think it sorts just stuff in tables, but that's not the case. It will sort list items or longer paragraphs either by the first word or by subsequent words (or by delimited fields) just as easily as table columns, for a whole file or a block of text you select, and it will sort on up to three different elements of an item at a time. Get it at Table, Sort (after making a selection, if you're not sorting the whole file). The options differ somewhat depending on what kind of material you're working with, so the best thing to do is open a garbage file and play with it.

The example in Chapter 1 uses Sort to get the citation copies into the same order as the reference section. The second-level sort is sometimes faster if you just horse the lines around with Cut and Paste (Ctrl+X and Ctrl+V), but the main Sort can also come in handy again here.

3.a–b

FIND AND REPLACE

To get at this most helpful facility, press Ctrl+H to open the Replace page of the Find and Replace dialog box, and then click the More button or press Alt+M to see the whole thing. (The stripped-down default version of this dialog box is another of Microsoft's stupider ideas, and there seems to be no way to make it open and display the whole thing every single time. But David Chinnell hocused up a little macro for me that runs automatically when Word opens, and does the job most of the time; see "Finding More Without Asking for It" in Chapter 8.) Explore the Format and Special buttons, which will give you a good idea of the kinds of things you can do beyond typing before and after text on the "Find what" and "Replace with" lines.

Note: Ctrl+F will open the Find page of the Find and Replace dialog box, but I recommend avoiding it if you're using Word 2002+. Another of the dis-enhancements introduced in that version is the option to highlight all items found—that is, to select them so you can copy them all at once or see them as you page through the file. That can be moderately useful—for collecting all the 1-heads for a nonautomated table of contents, for example—but the program-mers assigned it to Alt+T, the same hot key used to stop searching for specified formatting—meaning you have to press Alt+T *three times* instead of once to stop looking for formatting when you're using Find.

Word can (usually) find anything you can describe in a file, and replace it with anything you say you want, either one instance at a time or for a whole file, and you can even buy an add-in that will expand its efforts to a whole directory (see "Editorium Products" in Chapter 7). For example, use it for simple nui-sances like extra spaces. Hide the tracked changes (so Word doesn't keep finding spaces it already deleted), then

- *Find what:* [space][space] (meaning that you should type two spaces, not the words in the brackets or the brackets themselves)
- *Replace with:* [space]
- *Click:* Replace All (or press Alt+A) to do a *global change*, that is, to change every instance of two spaces to a single space without pausing so you can look at it

This might seem too basic to mention, but someone who's been a success-ful editor for *years* recently asked pretty much how to accomplish exactly this on one of the discussion lists where I hang out. (Actually, she asked how to get Word to get rid of double spaces after periods, which would be easy enough. In the example, just add a period at the beginning of the "Find what" and "Replace with" expressions. The broader expression is better, however, because modern typography no longer uses multiple spaces anywhere.) You may have to do this more than once, to eliminate the remains of triple spaces and other excesses. The white space special character (^w, where the ^ is the character above the 6 on most keyboards) is a bigger hammer—use it to get rid of all multiple spaces in one pass if you don't mind losing all your tabs at the same time.

At the other end of the scale, you can use Replace to install text that contains internal formatting—H_2O, for example, or *im*possible (which is what I used to think this trick was)—in one pass. Simply format one instance of the text the way you want to see it, then select it and press Ctrl+C to copy it to the Clipboard. Then set up the dialog like this:

- *Find what*: [the actual contents of the clipboard, or whatever other text you plan to replace with your formatting—water, for example]
- *Replace with*: ^c (the special character for the full contents of the Clipboard—say, H_2O—including the formatting, which won't normally show up in the dialog box)
- *Click*: Replace (or press Alt+R) to find and change one instance at a time, or Replace All (or press Alt+A) to do a global change

This trick works only in one direction; you can't use it to find specifically formatted text while ignoring strings of the same characters without formatting. Word refuses to take the ^c special character on the Find-what line.

You can also use Find and Replace for weirder and more complex things, feeding it *wildcards* (codes that look for classes of things or patterns rather than specific characters) and telling it to find all instances that fit the specified pattern, and then change something *next* to them while preserving the pattern itself.

For example, if you have a reference section where all the authors' initials are run together—A.B. Smith, C.D. Jones, and so on—and your client wants them spaced out, wildcard replace will let you go in and separate all the initials without putting a bunch of spaces where you don't want them. Here's how that would look:

- *Find what:* ([A-Z]).([A-Z])
- *Replace with:* \1.[space]\2 (again, using an actual space, not the word or the square brackets)
- *Check:* "Use wildcards" under "Search Options"

- *Click:* Replace (or press Alt+R) for each instance found

For a much better description of Word's wildcards than I have space for here, check out back issues of Jack Lyon's *Editorium Update* at www.editorium.com/euindex.htm. Look for the various discussions of wildcards under the "Finding and Replacing" heading.

One warning: Wildcards and Track Changes do not play well together, and it's usually necessary to turn off the latter to use the former successfully. That makes most global wildcard replace actions a whole lot scarier than I want to deal with; without the tracking, it's way too easy to miss the need to change something back if the operation "fixed" it improperly. So it's best to click the Replace button for each change you know you want unless things are very, very clear.

The example in Chapter 1 uses Find in a couple of different ways. When it talks about jumping from one citation to the next, what's actually happening is a search for open parentheses. Put a "(" on the "Find what" line and click the Find Next button, then press the Esc key to close the dialog box. Look for subsequent instances by pressing Ctrl+PageDown. *→ 1.b* This ploy takes advantage of the convention whereby almost every citation has a set of parentheses somewhere in it—either around the whole thing or just around the date. If the parens are being used for something other than a citation, just press Ctrl+PageDown again (or Ctrl+PageUp to go back if you run past a spot where you should have stopped).

Later, when the example talks about looking through files to find specific citations, you would get that effect by pasting *→ 4.b(3–6)* the author's name (or the whole citation) into the "Find what" line, then using that to search the indicated chapters for the citation in question.

The example also uses the Replace facility, first to separate groups of citations by replacing the semicolons and spaces that appear in citation clusters "(Smith, 1994; Jones, 2001; Abelskiver, 1984)" with hard returns:

- *Find what:* [semicolon][space]
- *Replace with:* ^p (the special character used in this tool to designate a paragraph break)

Then add the chapter numbers to the citations: *→ 2.*

- *Find what:* ^p

- *Replace with:* [space][chapter #]^p (again, leaving out the square brackets, and using the actual number of the chapter rather than the "chapter #" placeholder)

One more trick: If your author repeatedly confuses common words—*form* and *from,* for example, or *than* and *then* (or *that*)—use Find and Replace to flag the members of a pair with different colors. That will boost your chances of noticing when they're wrong, which is amazingly difficult while you're editing and dead easy for anyone just reading the material.

- *Find what:* [one of the problem words]
- *Check:* "Find whole words only"
- *Replace with:* [no text, Highlight] (that is, click More, Format, Highlight)
- *Click:* Replace all

Then go up to the Formatting toolbar, click the down arrow on the Highlight icon (the one with "ab" and a crayon, with a colored bar under it), pick another color, and repeat this Find and Replace operation for the other member of the pair. (If you don't see the icon, make sure you have the whole Formatting toolbar visible, as suggested under "Basic Survival Settings" in Chapter 2.) At the end of the job, select the whole file and set the highlighting to None.

Find and Replace is great stuff—but bear in mind that the original genie in a bottle has nothing on Word for literal-minded obedience, so you have to be very, very careful with it. The basic survival rule:

Never run a global change on a file you won't read again.

You don't want to find out in page proofs that fixing the author's obsessive use of *may* instead of the correct *can* has left things *canbe* happening on *Can* 15. And one sad drawback:

You can't completely trust Find.

Things sometimes happen in Word's innards to prevent it from finding things you can see on the screen, large as life and twice as ugly. Tracked changes can contribute to the problem but aren't the whole of it. Problems are much rarer with the latest versions of Word than they were a decade ago, but it feels like a good idea to warn you that it ain't perfect—if you ask it to find two consecutive spaces and it reports there aren't any, even though you can see some, well, you're right and it's wrong. Word happens. Don't worry about it—it really is rare. Think of it as one more reason the computer will stay a tool instead of trying to take over for you.

FILE SEARCH

"Didn't this author say something like this before, only different?"

Spatial memory is among the most refined and valuable skills of on-paper editing—the ability to know that something that bears on the edit at point B was first mentioned at point A ... two inches back up the stack of paper and about a third of the way down the page. Going straight to what you want is both admirable and pleasurable, and many a reluctantly electronic editor has bemoaned the impossibility of exercising this skill on screen, where it feels like you're peering through a toilet-paper roll at a tiny fragment of the manuscript.

The spatial part of spatial memory is gone; you really can't lay an eyeball on the whole manuscript. But the memory part still matters. When something makes you twitch, you can have your computer hunt through the manuscript files and tell you where the keywords you'd look for by eye on paper are to be found.

Exactly how you go about using this facility depends on your version of Word, and also on your operating system. In Word 2003, you can do it from File, File Search—a pane opens on the right with clear prompts, but I find it unspeakably tedious to use. Instead, I use Search in Windows Explorer (different from Internet Explorer; in Windows XP, get it at Start, All Programs, Accessories, Windows Explorer—and then put shortcuts wherever you think it'll be easier to get back to: Start, the desktop, the Quick Launch area). Highlight the directory containing the files you want to look through, click the Search button and then "All files and folders," paste the term you want to trace on the "Word or phrase in the file" line, and turn it loose. (You'd think it'd be faster to specify .doc files, since that's what you're looking for, but that option forces you into a second dialog to get to the search-for-text bit.) You can also open each file and use Find to search for the word or phrase; it's slower, but it works and may be easier to understand.

The example in Chapter 1 uses the file search facility to look for authors of sources that appear to be uncited in the text.   ✈ *4.b(4)*

GRAMMAR AND SPELLING CHECKERS

As it comes out of the box, Word (hyperhelpful as ever) wants to keep an eye on your grammar and your spelling for you and put squiggly lines of various colors under anything it thinks may be wrong. However, it also gives you the option of running the checkers on demand. I've turned all the real-time checking off—I want to think about spelling when I want to think about it, not when Word wants me to think about it—and I've also turned off the grammar checker entirely. (To control these settings, go to Tools, Options, Spelling & Grammar.)

Grammar Check Bad

Word can't *read*. It can only recognize some patterns of words, and the grammar checker is wrong more often than it's correct, both for what it identifies as an error and for what it proposes as a replacement. It's distinctly unsafe to consult the grammar checker unless your grasp of grammar is so solid that you really don't need it—and at that point, why bother? If you have particular things you want to look for—extra-long sentences, for instance—you can set up a custom grammar checker to look for just those and ignore everything else, but I haven't found even that worthwhile since I parted from the one client I knew would look at the statistics and judge the edit by them.

Spelling Check Good

The spelling checker, by contrast, is useful ... though still not entirely safe. All it can tell you is that a word is not in its dictionary, and then propose alternatives with similar spelling that it can find. That is, if the file says *tu*, Word will suggest *to* and *too* and *tub* and *tug* and a few others—but it can't tell which would be right, or even alert you when *tu* is correct for the Latin expression the author was quoting. (It does have some language settings other than English, but you'll rarely see them used in any way you'll find helpful unless you work in multilingual documents.)

I like to run the spelling checker just once, at the end of an edit or cleanup job, to catch things the naked eyeball missed plus any typos I inserted myself. Others prefer to run it twice, at the beginning and the end of a job, but that feels like extra work to me.

Run the spelling checker by pressing F7, then clicking the appropriate buttons in the dialog box (ignore the word flagged as an error; ignore all instances of that error; replace; and so on)—*after* you're sure what to do. For general vo-

cabulary, if none of the suggestions are obviously and unquestionably what the
file needs in place of what it already has, look up the word in the dictionary your
client specified for the job before you allow any change to the file. And even if
the word is valid, click Add to Dictionary only if it is something you know you'll
want to accept as a general rule, not just on the current job.

For names, click Ignore All each time they come up—but keep a mental
watch for names that should have come up already. The spelling checker can
alert you to subtle misspellings that you missed earlier. By the time you get to
the reference section, all the authors' names should pass the spelling checker. If
it stops on one that doesn't already have a query (that is, you have not yet asked
about a missing citation or misspelled name), that indicates a problem with the
spelling that you need to go back and look at again. (This works only if you
check all the spelling in one Word session; Word forgets the Ignore All stuff as
soon as you close the program. You can also make it forget what you've told it to
ignore and start over in a given session by clicking Recheck Document on Tools,
Options, Spelling & Grammar.)

Rearranging the Screen

Nothing's perfect. Even after you've got your screen environment—colors, typeface, spacing—to the optimal values for your eyes and approach to the job, you'll
still have places where you don't like what you see. It can be especially useful to
compress lists and tables to get more of the text onto the screen at a time. To
single-space a paragraph, press Ctrl+1 anywhere in it. You can also select larger
blocks of text and single-space them with the same built-in hot key. (Ctrl+2
double-spaces text.)

Also, if you're getting sleepy and can't afford to stop work for a break (which
is what you should do if at all possible), changing the length of the lines or the size
of the type will give you something refreshingly new to look at. (Press Ctrl+A to
select the whole file, then click File, Page Setup to change the margins. To change
the apparent size of the type, use Alt+V, Z or the zoom box on the Standard toolbar to make things larger or smaller on the screen. It can also help you wake up if
you switch from Normal view to Print Layout view or vice versa.)

The example in Chapter 1 uses several tricks to get the citation list into a form
that's easy to use. Select the whole thing, then shrink the type down
to 9 point (plenty readable with Lucida Console, though I wouldn't   3.c
recommend it for anything else), single-space the list, and use Format, Columns or the Columns icon on the Standard toolbar to make it use the
scratch paper more efficiently.

4 Deploying the Custom Features

Word isn't limited to the things you get when you open the box, or even to the choices it offers on the various option menus. You can change almost everything about it fairly easily—the trick is finding out what's possible. This chapter talks about the features most likely to come in handy for an editor.

Exclude Dictionary

As I say, Word can't read ... but you can make it come close. That is, you can compensate for the biggest drawback of the spelling checker—its willingness to accept anything in its dictionary, no matter how embarrassing, that looks sort of like the word you meant to use—by giving it a set of words you always want it to challenge. The last time I looked at it, my list had seventy-four words, ranging from the unpreferred (such as *advisor*; my clients all want *adviser* instead) to the unbearable (*asses* in place of *assess*, for instance). It's amazing how many *mangers of pubic works* and *marital arts instructors* this technique has spared the world!

Word 2003 includes good directions for setting up an exclude dictionary in its Help file, under "Specify a preferred spelling for a word." For info on using exclude dictionaries with earlier versions of Word, see the *Editorium Update* for December 5, 2001, at www.editorium.com/euindex.htm.

Your Own Keyboard

The stuff printed on the faces of the hundred-yumpty keys of your typical modern keyboard may seem like enough to keep track of, but Word comes out of the box with all sorts of other things hidden in various key combinations. A lot of what's there shows up in the menus, and it's a good idea to look at those combinations and learn the ones for the things you do most often—especially Ctrl+C (copy), Ctrl+X (cut), and Ctrl+V (paste), which you'll see on the Edit menu. The Insert, Symbol dialog box gives you the preprogrammed hot keys for special characters. And learn Ctrl+Z and Ctrl+Y—these are your basic get-out-of-trouble-free hot keys. The former will go back up Word's internal list of what you've done, one thing at a time, and wipe each one out as it gets to it; the latter will then go forward and put things back. Unfortunately, there's no way to skip anything in either direction; it's every step or none.

For a full list of the built-ins, point your browser to www.microsoft.com/en-able/products/keyboard.aspx (http://tinyurl.com/9lrja) and follow the prompts for your version of Word. (This charming site has the whole range of Microsoft shortcuts!) The function-key assignments are at the bottom of the list.

But there's more. Word really starts to fly when you put your own commands and choices on the keyboard, like the zippy little shortcut in Chapter 8 that sticks a comma ahead of the next *and* in the file (so you can make a serial comma happen from three lines away instead of mousing to the spot) or the one that turns a verb into a gerund.

The citation-checking example in Chapter 1 makes use of three hot-key combos. Two are for macros (described later); the third repeats the Find Next command. When I mentioned this under Find and Replace, I talk-ed about Ctrl+PageDown, the built-in hot key for this command, but in practice I don't use that one much, as it's relatively high on my keyboard and thus harder to reach than the bottom row. Instead, I've pro-grammed Ctrl+Num0 (the zero on the number pad) to find the next instance of whatever I'm looking for—in this case, an open paren.

At the moment, I have about fifty of these little jewels on my keyboard. How do I keep track? How do I even know how many there are? Simple: File, Print, Print What, Key Assignments. That sends your printer a list of all the tailored hot keys in Normal.dot and other templates currently active on the system.

To assign a hot-key combination, go to Tools, Customize, Keyboard, select a category (group of commands, macros, styles, or whatnot) in the panel on the left, then pick the item you want from the list on the right. Type the key combo you want to use in the "Press new shortcut key" box, then click Assign if it's safe. *Warning*: Most of the time, Word will tell you if your combo is already assigned to another task so you can decide if it's something you can afford to overwrite or not—but not always. Watch out for combos beginning with Alt; if you pair that key up with any of the letters that launch menus, Word will say "yes, boss!" and reassign the combo, leaving you stuck using the mouse to get to the menu. (It's easy enough to delete the customization and thereby restore the original command when the problem surfaces, but I always feel like such a doofus when I forget....)

TOOLBARS AND MENUS

The toolbars and menus that come with Word are reasonably useful—especially after you go into Tools, Customize, Options and set the Standard and Format-ting toolbars on two lines, as recommended for basic survival in Chapter 2. In addition, two relatively obscure built-in items—one menu and one toolbar— can make life a lot easier.

The Work menu provides a place to park shortcuts to files you use all the time. It works like the recently opened file list on the File menu, giving you a push-down numbered list of up to nine files, but you designate the files to appear there, and they stay on the list until they get pushed off the bottom, unless you pull them off first. Find it at Tools, Customize, Commands, Built-in Menus (it's the last item on the list) and drag it up to the menu bar to start using it.

The Function Key toolbar lists the commands currently on F1 through F12, and it changes when you press Alt, Shift, and Ctrl to show what the F keys do with the auxiliary keys pressed. Find it at Tools, Customize, Toolbars; check Function Key Display.

And Tools, Customize has a lot more to offer. The dialogs there will allow you to hang any command you want—and any macro you have on your system—onto any menu or toolbar, pull anything now on a toolbar or menu off of it, and even make menus and toolbars of your own. All it takes is dragging and dropping items from the Tools, Customize, Commands lists to the toolbars and menus. Dead easy. If it doesn't work intuitively from this description, check the relevant back issues of the *Editorium Update* (www.editorium.com/euindex. htm), under "Customization."

Voice Controls: Look, Ma, No Hands!

Word 2002+ comes with a speech engine flexible enough to be a big help to the working editor. In Voice Command mode, it will run all the menu commands, plus many of the keyboard and mouse commands—including Page Up and Page Down, Delete and Backspace, and Select Word, Sentence, or Paragraph. And it will run your macros, too, if you list them on a toolbar of their own and teach the engine their names.

To get started with speech processing, plug a microphone into your computer and get it working. It doesn't have to be anything special; I'm using the $40 Labtec desk stand mike I bought for my Windows 95 computer back around 1999, mounted on a sort of Rube Goldberg contraption that puts the head right beside my mouth.

Then go to Word's Tools menu and click Speech. What? Speech? Yes, it's there. For five years, I didn't see it either. Anyway, Word will reply by asking for its CD, as the speech engine isn't part of the standard installation. Once you put in the CD, Word will pull in the files it needs and open a tutorial. (Nothing will happen to your other settings.) Figure on working through at least three or four of the training pieces eventually; you don't have to do it all at once, but the more you read to Word, the better the recognition you will get.

You can find a list of the built-in speech commands on the Microsoft Web site, at http://office.microsoft.com/en-us/word/HA010348831033.aspx (http://tinyurl.com/3me9nq). Instructions for making Word execute macros by voice command are at http://office.microsoft.com/en-us/word/HA010348911033.aspx (http://tinyurl.com/4d899m).

Word 2007 also has voice processing available to it, using a speech engine that is said to be even better than the one in Word 2003, which is the only one I've played with.

Macros

A macro is a way of storing a bunch of instructions for your computer, so you can get the effect you want by asking for it rather than going through all the steps. It's sort of like the difference between phoning for a pizza and digging out all the ingredients and the baking stone to make your own, but with the advantage that what you get is your own recipe and not Pizza Hut's; you just don't have to do the work.

Sample Application

The citation-checking example in Chapter 1 makes use of two macros—the ones called "Fillerup" and "GetThat" in Chapter 8. The first starts at the insertion point and selects everything through the next closing parenthesis—allowing you to pick up authors' names whether they're inside the parens with the date or not. The second takes the selected text, copies it onto another document (I use the end of the style sheet for this), moves to a new line there, returns to the main document, finds the next open parenthesis, and stops immediately to its right. If that turns out to be the beginning of a citation, all I have to do is hit the Fillerup combo again, followed by the GetThat combo— respectively Ctrl+Shift+[semicolon] and Ctrl+[semicolon] on my system. Otherwise, I either move the insertion point to the real   ✈ *1.b* beginning and proceed as before, or press the hot keys for Find Next.

More Help with Macros

Like most of Word's extra goodies, macros are easy to start working with but have endless possibilities. You don't have to be a programmer to use them: simply learn to record them (Tools, Macro, Record new macro). For a guided practice session that will take you from the simplest introduction to fairly giddy heights in a couple of hours, point your Web browser to www.powersedit.com/ftp/macrofiles.zip. Unzip the archive, print out the file called "Handout," and follow its directions for the rest.

TEMPLATES

Word always uses a separate file called a *template* to govern the appearance of a document and set up the working environment. If you don't tell it to use something else, what you get is a template called "Normal.dot," which provides a generic set of styles and formatting information and sets up basic menus and toolbars for you. If you want anything different—your own AutoText and hot keys, your own menus and toolbars or extra items on the standard-issue set, your own choice of fonts and styles—you either change Normal.dot or build a new template, or you do some of both.

Updating Normal.dot is both the easiest and the riskiest course of action. It's easiest because everything you might do defaults to Normal.dot; it takes additional steps to make something go anywhere else. But because Normal.dot is always grinding along in the background, it's exposed to random damage—making it virtually certain that one day it will turn toes-up and Word will stop working properly. Its constant use also makes it a preferred target of virus writers. If (when) it goes out of action, it's not the end of the world; all you have to do is close Word, delete or rename Normal.dot, and restart. Word will create a nice new all-default Normal.dot for you, and you'll be back in business ... without your customizations. (See "Simple Insanity" in Chapter 6 for more on digging out of Word trouble; regenerating Normal.dot is just one of several possibilities, and not the first one to try.)

Using Templates

I take a mixed approach to the use of templates. For things I know I'll want no matter whose stuff I'm working on, I go ahead and update Normal.dot. Then I make a copy of the file: go to File, Open, Look in [the directory where the templates are kept, which varies depending on the version of Word in use and any special instructins Word has been given] and double-click Normal.dot—which opens happily even though it's in use—and save a copy: File, Save As, Norm-BakMMDDYY.dot (where "MMDDYY" represents today's date).

For Word 2002+, the default location for your templates is C:\Documents and Settings\[your username]\Application Data\Microsoft\Templates. If this path doesn't seem to exist on your computer, go to Windows Explorer and click Tools, Folder Options, View. Adjust the check boxes so Windows will show you everything. At minimum, make sure to set the "Show hidden files and folders" radio button, and to *un*check "Hide extensions for known file types" and "Hide protected operating system files"—even though the latter is "Recommended." Earlier versions of Word will probably keep templates in C:\Program Files\Microsoft Office\Templates. You can tell you're in the right place when you see a file called "Normal.dot"—or just "Normal" on a Mac. (*Note*: It turns out that Word doesn't actually care where you keep your templates. At Tools, Options, File Locations, you can designate any location you please for the regular templates, including Normal.dot, and for the ones with macros designed to run once, when Word starts up. On my new computer, my data files are on a separate physical disk from my programs and operating system, and I keep both templates and startup files there now, at D:\WordUserTemplates and D:\WordStartup. Creating those folders has made life much simpler.)

I keep several editions of Normal.dot, so I can always go back to a good copy. If I have to kill it, rather than let Word build me a new one, I simply copy the most recent backup, name it Normal.dot, and go on my way—and if that one doesn't work for some reason, I can go back to an earlier one.

For the rest, I have two sets of templates. One is for pure formatting; templates in this group contain nothing but style decisions—what fonts and sizes and line spacing and margins to use for different elements. When I start work on a job, I attach an edit-friendly style template to the files. Then at the end of the job, I attach a template that makes the file look like what the client wants to see, which keeps everyone happy. I use macros for both operations, but it's quite easy to do manually—just click Attach in the top half of the Tools, Templates and Add-ins dialog to get a list of the available templates, and then double-click the template you want to use. Check "Automatically update document styles" on this dialog to make the text in your document take on the appearance specified for styles of the same names in the new template. (*Note*: Word has another auto-update option, at Format, Style, Modify—but that one will drive you mad. Do not check it unless you really want anything you do to a bit of text—italicize a word, say—to propagate back to the style and any styles based on it.)

The other template set is for macros and toolbars and menus, all designed so that I can do the same things on every job but get different effects based on what each client wants. When I work on a job, I use the bottom half of the Tools, Templates and Add-ins dialog to load a global template (a template available to all Word files) designed for that specific client—called, unenterprisingly enough, "my[Client].dot"—that handles a variety of standardizable chores. For example, these days everyone wants a copyeditor working on screen to do typemarking of some sort and put in queries to the author—but the formatting of the typemarking and the queries will differ dramatically from client to client. To take first-level heads, for example, my clients all want some combination of these approaches:

- Standard Word style "Heading 1" or client-specific Word style with a different name or "Normal" (which is as close as Word gets to no style at all)
- Typemarking code of @H1: or [H1] or <1> or <A> or no code at all
- Followed at the beginning of the next paragraph by @TX: or [TX L] or <GT> or no code at all (and perhaps also an unindented style or nothing else)
- And followed in the second paragraph by yet another code and a tab or a different style that includes an indentation decision—or not

I don't want to use brainpower to keep track of that sort of thing, so every myClient template includes a macro that does whatever that client wants for a first-level head, and every myClient template has that macro assigned to Alt+1. When I perceive the need to typemark something as a first-level head, I press Alt+1, and Word provides whatever permutations of codes and styles that client has requested, then moves the insertion point to the beginning of the first line of paragraph text—after the typemarking code, if any.

For queries I take the same approach—every myClient template has a user menu called Queries (constructed as described earlier under "Toolbars and Menus," with the Q key hot), and the first item on every Queries menu is a query to the author. That takes advantage of the way Word deals with menus—when you activate a menu from the keyboard, the first item on it is automatically selected, so that's what you get if you just press Enter after opening the menu. That means Alt+Q, Enter gets me a query to the author; Alt+Q, 2 (no need to press Enter) gets me a query to the production editor, and then the list starts to vary by special things different clients tell me they need.

Template Hierarchy

So Word uses templates to define styles and menus and all sorts of stuff. ... How does it tell what template to consult at any given point? When you just stick with Normal.dot, it's simple—that's the only template in play, and everything comes from there. But the system I'm recommending always has at least three templates active at the same time. Here's how they fight it out:

1. The template attached to the file (via Tools, Templates and Add-ins, Attach—the top half of the dialog box) governs anything it addresses.

2. Then the current global templates (the ones you've instructed Word to list in the bottom half of the Tools, Templates and Add-ins dialog box by clicking Add there, and then checked off to indicate you want them right now) do their thing. If two of them try to use the same hot key, Word sits there and sneers at you when you press the key—so make sure you keep your keyboard settings distinct for any templates you might want to use at the same time.

3. Normal.dot plays cleanup. Anything Word needs to know that isn't specified in the attached or global templates comes from Normal.dot—either the built-in defaults or whatever modifications you've made to them.

More Help with Templates

Like macros, templates have too many ramifications to cover properly in a book of this size. For a guided practice that will take you through enough of the basics to use them comfortably, point your Web browser to www.powersedit.com/ftp/ templatefiles.zip. Unzip the archive, print out the file called "Handout," and follow its directions for the rest.

5 DOMESTICATING TRACKED CHANGES

O f everything Word offers to an aspiring editor, Track Changes probably evokes the most angst. It makes the screen look funny. It interferes with other aspects of using Word. It either imitates an accident in a paint factory or makes it almost impossible to tell who did what. It rats you out if you work at midnight or on weekends instead of standard office hours. What's an editor to do?

Suck it up.

With some minor care and adjustment of the settings, Track Changes is great stuff. You can reduce the look-funny factor a lot by the way you make each change; you can turn it off when it's going to make something else sick; you can (alas) get used to its peculiar color choices—or refresh them when they're too awful; you can ignore or hocus the time stamps. (I've never had any client mention them, but if one did, I'd just say, "Yes, I work odd hours. That's the advantage of being a freelancer." If push comes to shove, you can change the clock so the time stamps show what the client wants to see … but I'd have serious reservations about the value of a client who needed that sort of babying.)

Note: Track Changes differs a lot from one version of Word to the next. Before Word 2002, the options for what to track and where to show the results are on the Tools menu, under Track Changes in the more recent editions and Revisions in the earlier ones; in Word 2002+, all of that is on the Reviewing toolbar (View, Toolbars, Reviewing). The concepts stay pretty much the same, though, as long as you don't decide to play with balloons. The following discussion focuses on Word 2003.

SETTINGS

The main thing to remember about your Track Changes setup is that it's *yours*— no choice you make on Tools, Options, Track Changes will have any effect whatsoever on any other machine. Use balloons or not, if your version of Word has them. (Mine does, but I don't like them, so I keep them turned all the way off.) Format the tracking so you feel most comfortable. (Or least uncomfortable.)

But unless you're the only one who will make tracked changes to the files you work on, do not pick a specific color. It looks as though you ought to be able to pick one of those wonderful colors for your own stuff and let your authors pick theirs, but that ain't how it works. If you pick a color, every tracked change—yours, your author's, your production editor's cat's—will show up in that color. (On your machine, if you like it, do it; it makes no never mind to anyone else. I use the dark red on my travel computer, where I'm almost always editing rather than dealing with author reviews, and where I'm often in lighting conditions that make Word's default color choice hard on the eyes.)

The only way to have Word clearly differentiate one reviewer from another is to set the colors for additions and deletions to "By author"—the boxes on Tools, Options, Track Changes that show up as half red and half blue. That does the job, but it turns you over to the Surprise Party Department in the process.

Here's how it works: Every time you start Word, that's a new session, and in each session, the author of the first change Word encounters is assigned the color red. That's why your own work is almost always red, and you might be tempted to go for something gentler, say green. ... The next author discovered to have changed anything anywhere almost always gets blue. After that, it's unpredictable for another seven colors, some of which—the goose-turd yellow and electric magenta in particular—are downright nasty, while others, like the regular green and the dark red, are quite pleasant. And if you should be so fortunate as to have a tenth reviewer in play during a session, just to put the cherry on top, number ten gets red again.

If the colors start to double up or a high-volume contributor to a file gets a color you hate to look at, just close Word and reopen it, and then open a different file first. That will get you a new array of color assignments, quite possibly easier to live with, and you'll be OK as long as all ten-plus reviewers aren't messing with the same file. ... Alternatively, you can pick a color (knowing that it will apply to everyone) and hover the mouse pointer over any change where you want to know the source; if you have Tools, Options, View set to show Screen-Tips, a little box will appear indicating who made the change and when.

Besides the colors, you can control the onscreen appearance of the typeface used for insertions, deletions, and formatting changes, and also the location of the *change bars*—the vertical lines in the margin that indicate whether anything in the corresponding lines of text has been changed. I like boldface insertions, strikeover deletions, no flag for formatting, and change bars in the left margin, but you can set these values to whatever you find congenial, secure in the knowledge that no one else will see what you have decided to do.

If you're using Word 2002+, you have one more place to look: On Tools, Options, Security, make sure the check box labeled "Make hidden markup visible when opening or saving" is checked. That way, you will see tracking if it exists in any file you open, and your files will all be tagged as having been saved with the tracking visible—meaning that they'll open in that state on computers running earlier versions of Word, which are set to show or hide revisions at open based on their status last time someone saved the file.

KEEPING THE SCREEN SANE

A comfortable author is a happy author, and a happy author makes for a happy editor. The way your tracked changes look can boost or lower your author's happiness level in a big way, so it's well worth taking a bit of extra care to keep the screen as simple, uncluttered, and easy to read as you can. Figure 2 illustrates the techniques you can use to do this, and the following sections discuss them in more detail.

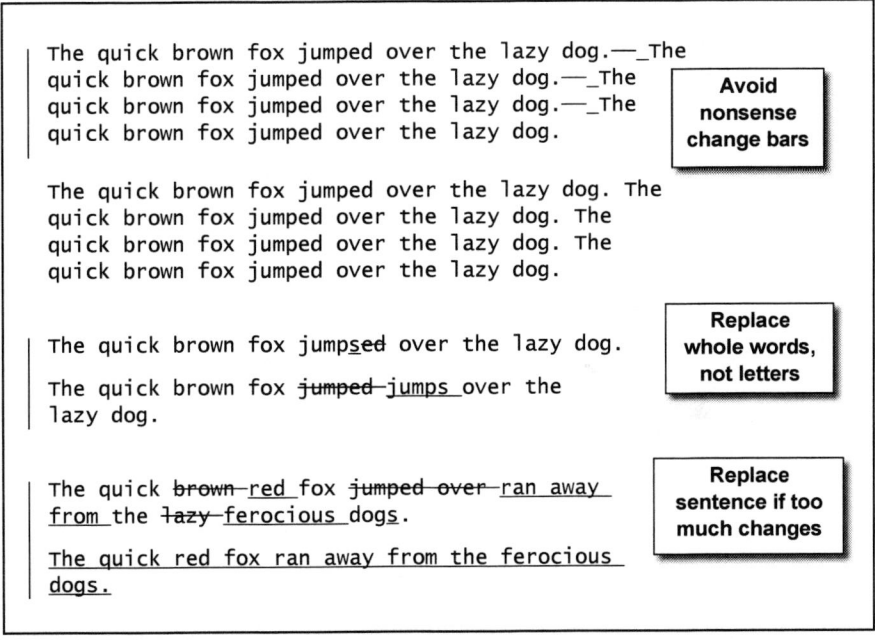

Figure 2. Taming the Tracking

When Nobody Cares, Nobody Cares

Publishers tend to require lots of corrections that don't change the semantic content of a manuscript. Things like the number of spaces between sentences, the spacing between paragraphs, the punctuation of quotes, and a raft of other mechanical things need to be set quite precisely for the page-makeup program, but they're not something the author should be concerned about.

So what you want to do is take them right out of play. If your client agrees, make all such changes with the tracking turned off, so the author isn't presented with page after page of change bars flagging things that need no attention. It's useful to skim the files at the beginning of a job to get an idea of the extent of this sort of thing, and to pick up on the more egregious typewriter relics: use of the spacebar instead of the tab key to line up tables, for example. That way you can plan your attack and take care of as much as possible up front.

Ideally, you want to turn the tracking on once *and leave it on.* If you keep it running but invisible, which often makes the edit much more congenial, it's amazingly easy to flip it off to deal with one little thing and then realize half an hour later that it's still off. (A point I'm reminded of forcibly all too often; I had to apply the last-ditch advice from the "Restoring Lost Tracking" section in this chapter on a live job shortly after I wrote it.)

Make It Logical

When you're working on paper, it's logical up to a point to change the smallest error—for example, delete the *ed* at the end of a verb that ought to be in the present tense and replace it with *s*—but eventually it's better to just cross out the whole word and replace it. Likewise for a sentence with several words changed, and very occasionally even for a paragraph that's been well and truly carved up.

It's the same on the screen, but the point comes much sooner—replacing the entire logical unit (especially a word) is almost always easier on the author, and it needn't make noticeably more work for the editor. Two tricks make all the difference:

- *On Tools, Options, Edit, check "Typing replaces selection":* Then build the habit of selecting letters you want to replace in a word rather than backspacing over them or deleting them. It takes no more effort; the extra key press (Shift+arrow to select, as opposed to Backspace or Delete alone) is more than balanced by the layout of the keyboard—the Shift and arrow keys are easier to get to than Backspace or Delete. But when you select part of a word to change instead of erasing the letters, you get a whole new word, not just the letters you type, and that is much easier to read.
- *Record a simple macro to replace a selection with itself:* This is one of the easiest to build and most useful tools you can have, and all it takes is selecting any text, then turning on the macro recorder and pressing Ctrl+X (cut) followed by Ctrl+V (paste). Turn off the recorder and give the macro a hot key—I use Ctrl+R for Replace—and use it whenever a sentence

gets hard to read because too many words have changed. You can also use it at the paragraph level—but sparingly, and just where you want the author to think about the whole statement as opposed to its parts. (For more on macros, read the "Macros" section of Chapter 4.)

Remember Case

Word offers a handy-dandy command called ChangeCase that acts as a three-way toggle, changing words or selected text from lowercase to initial caps to all caps and back around to lowercase. It defaults to Shift+F3, but it's so useful that I also keep it on Ctrl+[slash] so it's right under my hand. However, it has one, ah, feature that makes it even more useful or too dangerous to use, depending on what you're working on: *Track Changes cannot see it.*

So if the author has misused case in ways that are utterly uncontroversial and not subject to question, you can use ChangeCase to normalize the text without crudding up the manuscript with a bunch of extra tracking. But. If the author's use of case might matter, keep your fingers off this shortcut. At least on the first appearance of a term that may need reevaluation, make the edit by selecting the initial letter and typing over it in the other case. That will get you the old form of the word wholly deleted and the new one wholly added, making it much harder to miss. Then put in a query explaining the change to the author and asking if it's acceptable—and promising to fix it if it's not. (Whether to make subsequent changes blind—without tracking them—or not is a judgment call. You have to weigh the amount of work you save up front against the amount of hassle to find all the little devils later if it turns out you have to go back to them.)

Abandoning the Toolbar

The Reviewing toolbar (like the equivalent dialogs in earlier versions of Word) is part and parcel of Word's oh-you-poor-dear-let-me-take-care-of-you approach to its users. On it, you can indeed do everything you might need to do with regard to tracked changes: move from revision to revision, accept and reject changes, adjust the kinds of things you see on the screen. But it's slow and cumbersome, requiring you to mouse around instead of keeping your hands on the keyboard.

Rather than waste screen real estate on the whole thing, I've added the four items I find useful—Display for Review, Show, Accept Change, and Reject Change—to the Standard toolbar in my Normal.dot. Display for Review provides a quick reminder of the status of the system, while Show lets me control which reviewers' work and what kinds of changes appear on the screen. The

Accept and Reject buttons rarely come in handy, but I've used them (mainly the former) in concert with Show to clear other people's revisions while leaving my own in the tracking. For the rest, moving from change to change during an edit review is easy enough by eye with the movement keys, augmented by Find, because you never want to stop at each and every change—just the ones you need to do something about individually. And I never use Word Comments, so I don't need those buttons at all. I use hot keys for most of the functions of the Reviewing toolbar:

- *Turn Track Changes on and off:* Ctrl+Shift+E (a built-in hot key)
- *Turn the display of tracking off while keeping Track Changes running:* Ctrl+Shift+Alt+[comma] (my own hot key; runs a recorded macro)
- *Turn the display of tracking on while keeping Track Changes running:* Ctrl+Alt+[comma] (my own hot key; runs a recorded macro)
- *Approve a selected change:* Alt+[period] (my own hot key; runs a recorded macro)
- *Reject a selected change:* Alt+[comma] (my own hot key; runs a recorded macro)
- *Approve all changes remaining in a file:* Shift+Alt+[backtick; the lowercase character under the tilde] (my own hot key; runs a recorded macro)

Note: I used to use just Alt+[backtick] for approving residual changes, but it was too easy to hit as a typo for Alt+1. In addition, I used to make a lot of use of the "Accept Change" button to clear changes in formatting, but I finally got a clear-tracked-format macro working—see Chapter 8.

Moving Text Without Losing the Tracking

Sometimes you get a paragraph or so properly edited, only to realize that it really belongs somewhere else in the manuscript. Then you discover that if you cut and paste, you lose all the details; the original shows up as deleted, and the new location just has the edit. The solution depends on your version of Word.

In 2000+, all you have to do is turn off Track Changes (in both files, if you're moving something from one file to another). Cut and paste, and all the tracking will come along. Of course, the paragraph will otherwise look as though it was always in the new spot and never in the old one, so it's a good idea to add tracked notes to the author at both points, explaining what got moved and where.

Word 97 has a bug that prevents this from working; the Clipboard just can't see tracking. Assuming that's not reason enough to upgrade, here's how you get around it: Select the whole passage you want to move, then go to Insert, Bookmark and put in a bookmark name. Save the file (under a new name if you're moving text within a file), and then move the insertion point to the place you want to put the text. Make sure Track Changes is off in the target file. Open the File, Insert dialog and enter the name of the bookmarked file in the "File Name" box and the bookmark name in the "Range" box. Word will insert the captured text in the new location, track marks and all. Turn Track Changes back on, and remember to delete the captured text from its original location if you don't want it in both places.

Restoring Lost Tracking

Murphy rules. If you ever allow yourself to stop the tracking "just for a moment," you will eventually forget to turn it back on again at the end of the moment. What you do next depends on how much work you did before you spotted the goof.

If it's just a paragraph or so, you're probably best off pressing Ctrl+Z (Undo) repeatedly until you get back to the last edit that you tracked, then turning on the tracking and repeating the work. If your memory is like mine or if you've done enough work to overload your memory, that will be more of a chore than you're likely to want to deal with from scratch; in that case, before you start undoing things, make a copy of the edit you forgot to track and paste it into a new document so you can use it as a guide for the replacement.

For a longer lapse, your only friend is Compare and Merge Documents—and it ain't that much of a friend. It looks like a good idea:

1. Save the edited file, then Save As a copy, approve all changes in it, and close the copy.

2. Make a new copy of the untouched original, clear any tracking that the author may have left in it, and rerun any changes you deliberately made without tracking them—spacing and format changes and whatnot. (If you find you need to do this often, make a habit of keeping an interim set of files that include only the untracked changes to the originals.)

3. Go to Tools, Compare and Merge Documents and follow the prompts, identifying your edit copy as the Compare target.

If you have lived a truly virtuous life, the active document, now bearing the name of the edit copy, will appear on your screen with all the changes tracked in the right direction (things removed from the original showing as deleted, and new stuff showing as added). Once you confirm that this version of the file is usable, you can save it and then rename it so it's the primary edit file. Alternatively, you can manually copy the changes into the copy of the file you were working on when you noticed the lapse.

Why would you do this manually? Unfortunately, Compare is a fragile and fractious beast. It easily gets lost and starts designating huge swatches of text as added or deleted, losing all the internal detail. That's doubly true if one editor or reviewer has edited another person's edits. And you won't catch all the blind changes, no matter how hard you try; if nothing else, Compare is sensitive to the ChangeCase alterations that Track Changes doesn't spot.

If the reconstituted copy is too awful to use, you have one more chance:

1. Make a copy of the untracked part of the edit and paste it into a new file.
2. Make a copy of the corresponding part of the original—using the one you prepared for the first Compare effort—and paste it into yet another new file.
3. Run the comparison again, working from the partial copy of the original to the partial copy of the edit. With less input, Compare has a better chance of working properly.
4. If you get a usable passage, make sure Track Changes is turned off in the marked-up file and the full edit file, then paste the text over the edit you forgot to track. Don't forget to turn Track Changes on again!

And if it's still too full of garbage to show the author, all you can do is decide whether it's worse to redo the work or apologize for losing the tracking....

Protecting Tracked Changes

So you put your twenty or forty or eighty hours into making the very best edit you can ... and then you send the files back to the author. That's gotta be scary. (At least as scary as it was for the author to send it off for editing, but that's another story.) What if the author just gets rid of everything you did? Or even some of it?

Many publishers still avoid this issue by sending authors only a printout of the edited files. The author marks up the hard copy by hand—providing any extensive changes on disk if the editor responsible for processing the author review is very, very fortunate—and someone sits down when it comes back and types, scans, or otherwise inputs all the changes.

But if the author does get the files back—and more and more do—it's useful to do something to try to make sure the edit doesn't just disappear, either accidentally or deliberately. Once again, Word is there to help. Sort of.

What Word does is allow you to "protect the file for tracked changes," which prevents anyone from turning off the Track Changes facility. I use the macros given in Chapter 8 for this, but you can do it directly on a file by clicking Tools, Protect. In the task pane that opens on the right side of the screen, check the box under "2. Editing restrictions," then select "Tracked changes" in the drop-down list that becomes accessible. When you click the Yes box under "3. Start enforcement," Word will open a dialog box for setting a password. (You can skip the password if you prefer, but in that case anyone can just turn the protection off again.) Protection for tracked changes also disables the approval and rejection buttons on the Reviewing toolbar.

With the file protected for tracked changes, the author can still add or delete text, but apparently only out in the open—the regular tools that would allow changes to disappear or be done blind don't work. If you decide to go this route, the main worry is forgetting or mistyping the password; the macros in Chapter 8 will allow you to automate the process, so you never get it wrong.

When you discuss protection with your authors, stop here.

Publisher clients generally request protection, so the authors have no beef with you, and you can persuade most private clients that the protection helps them make sure they don't inadvertently lose their investment in the edit. (Which is true; it's the author's book, and an author who's buying an edit can insist on any text at all—there's no need to sneak.)

But in fact, protection for tracked changes is a sham. If you wind up with a protected file, you need to kill the tracking, and you *don't* have the password, here's what you do:

1. Use your hot keys (the ones with recorded macros) to process the review and incorporate the author's changes. That is, reject any of your edits that the author wants to get rid of, delete the queries, and approve and edit any new text the author wants to add. Ignore any edits the author accepts.
2. Use the hot key with the macro that approves everything else to clear the rest of the edit.
3. Copy all the text in the file.
4. Open a new blank file and paste in the text.
5. Close the original file, then rename it.
6. Save the copy under the original name.

Removing Tracking from an Edited File

The big strength of Track Changes is the way it eliminates the need to retype accepted edits in the final version of the file. Once you address all the points the author raises about an edit, adjusting or removing changes as needed and erasing any queries you've put into the file, you can approve everything else holus-bolus and go your way rejoicing.

Well, almost. It's unfortunately easy to screw up the spacing around tracked changes, leaving too many or too few spaces or lines around places where changes were tracked in the file. Many of the resulting problems will surface in a final run of the spelling checker, so you should always do that *after* clearing the tracking. But—yet more unfortunately—the spelling checker won't catch everything. To get at the things it misses, I run three wildcard searches on each file, looking at each hit to see if it's OK or not. (They can't be cleared globally, because some of the things each one finds will be correct already, and the ones that aren't may need different corrective actions at different points in the file.) Here are my three "Find what" strings:

- .[! ^013'"0-9\)<\[\]]
- [!0-9^013•]^t
- ^013[!^t\@•]

These strings assume that your client is using typemarking codes to identify formatting elements, including basic text, and that paragraph indentation employs tab characters. If you use them, type in everything here, including the square brackets, and remember to select the "Use wildcards" check box in the Find and Replace dialog box. The first string finds periods that are not followed by spaces, hard returns, quotes, numbers, closing parens, open angle brackets, or square brackets (either open or closed). The second finds tabs not preceded by numbers, hard returns, or bullets (the character produced by typing Alt+0149), and the third finds hard returns that are not followed by tabs, @ signs (used to delimit typemarking codes by my main client), or bullet characters. I keep them all in AutoCorrect, using "!3" (which I read as *not-three*, for the three negatives they chase) as the trigger. To use them, I type "!3" at the beginning of the first manuscript file and let AutoCorrect put them onto the page, then cut and paste them one by one into the "Find what" line of a wildcard search. After I've searched that file for all three, making any adjustments that are needed, I close the file and repeat the searches one after another on each of the other files, taking advantage of the down arrow beside the "Find what" line to restore earlier search strings.

6 Coping with Snares and Pitfalls

For an editor, Word comes close to Churchill's definition of democracy: the worst system available, except for all the others. It has towering strengths—but great weaknesses and problems as well. Here's the cream of the crud—and what to do about it.

Note: Much of this chapter discusses Word in the context of a program called WordPerfect—which, if you've come to computers in the past decade, you've probably never seen and may barely have heard of. Obscure as it may seem, the background offers some useful insights into the behavior of Word—the tool most clients insist we use—and I commend it to your attention. However, if you've no interest in this aspect of history, you needn't read it—just skip from "Why Word Can't Reveal Codes" to "Master Documents" and go on from there. Some of the remaining sections of the chapter mention WordPerfect briefly, but they mainly address deficiencies and work-arounds in Word.

Simple Insanity

Word sometimes goes bonkers. That is, some or all of the menus and commands suddenly stop getting the effects you've learned to love (or at least expect) and instead do other things entirely. What have you done wrong?

Nothing.

What caused the fit? In the computer's working memory and in the file itself lurk forty-two gazillion electronic whatsits whose state must be exactly what it's supposed to be, and any of which can make a program or an individual file "behave unpredictably" (computer-speak for "look all screwed up") if it gets out of whack. So when things do behave unpredictably, chances are that somewhere in its little insides, your computer has lost its place, and messages and commands meant for one bit of software are reaching another.

When unintended results appear, waste no time figuring out exactly what's wrong—anything you see is almost certainly just a symptom of a generic problem with a generic fix:

1. Press Esc. Often, the Escape key is all it takes to restore Word to a sense of its duty. If that doesn't work ...

2. Close Word and reopen it. Open the file you were working on. If it's back to normal, you're home and dry.

3. If it's not, open another file. If *it's* normal, skip to step 5. If both files are screwed up, close Word and rename your Normal.dot file. Reopen Word, letting it generate a new, all-default Normal.dot. If Word is still misbehaving, go on to step 4. If Word is OK with a default Normal.dot and you have a customized backup of Normal.dot from before the problem started, close Word again, make a copy of your last good backup (*not* the one you just renamed), name the copy "Normal.dot," then restart Word and go your way rejoicing.

4. Close Word and the rest of the programs you have open, then restart your computer and open Word again. Check both misbehaving files. If they're both OK now, you're back in business, except that if you had a customized Normal.dot file, you'll probably want to close Word one more time, delete the Normal.dot file you'll find in the template directory, and restart with a renamed copy of the last good Normal.dot backup. If the *warm boot* didn't fix things, shut everything down, including your operating system, turn off your computer, and wait sixty seconds. Turn it on and try again (a *cold boot*). If the second file you opened is not back to normal, go to step 7. If it's OK but the original file is still screwed up, go to step 5.

5. See whether inserting the file leaves the garbage behind. Open a new blank file, with the tracking turned off. Make sure the tracking is also turned off in the problem file, close it, and use Insert, File to put a copy into the new file. Save it under a new name, close it, and reopen it; if it's back to normal, save it under the working name and you're done. If not, go on to step 6.

6. *Maggie* the misbehaving file. That is, turn on the display of hidden text so you can see the paragraph marks, then select and copy everything in the file except the very last paragraph mark. Open a new blank file and paste in what you just copied, then close the new file, saving it under a new name. Close the old file. Open the new one. If it's OK, you're clear, and you can save it under the working name. If it's not, repeat the procedure one section at a time, copying everything up to each section break except for the last paragraph mark in a section. If any of the copied sections are still misbehaving, repeat the procedure on them one paragraph at a time (or divide them in half if they have lots of paragraphs, and keep subdi-

viding until you've isolated the problem). If so much is misbehaving that there seems no end to the trouble, go to step 7.

Note: Word 2003 is more sensitive to corruption than earlier versions—but in a good way. It detects subtle problems that prior editions would have tried to work with and refuses to open the file normally. At that point, you can often get a cure by using the Open and Repair option, available on the down arrow in the lower right corner of the File, Open dialog.

And if *that* doesn't work (or you've a yen to see more of the history of a file than its author probably wants you to see), go to File, Open and set "Files of type" to "Recover Text from Any File." That will lose all the formatting in the file but will at least extract the text—and at the end, you'll see all the metadata the file has accumulated, including who saved it and on what version of Word. To keep the results of this maneuver, you need to Save the file deliberately (under the old name or a new one); Word doesn't offer to save the file for you if you just close it.

7. Yell for help. Specify the version of Word you're using and the operating system, and be as clear as you can about what seems to be wrong and what you've done about it. If framing that message doesn't make you smack your forehead and fix the error yourself, and your usual sources of help run dry, try one of the sources listed in Chapter 7.

I tend to apply the process in this order because—given the number of programs I keep open all the time—I really hate to shut down the computer. But the whole thing is worth trying before making the slightest effort to see if you might have done something wrong yourself—that is, something that makes Word produce the peculiar results you see by obeying your instructions—which is the kind of thing you're apt to find out when you call for help.

MAGIC MENU DESTRUCTION TOOL

Parts of Word were built by developers for developers, and some of the little helpers left by that process are not safe for any ordinary mortal to deal with. The worst offender is what I call the Magic Menu Destruction tool, which will pull anything off a menu with a single click, no confirmation required.

If ever you see the mouse pointer change from a thin vertical bar to a fat horizontal one, freeze. Get your hands off the pointing device, and then reach out and press the Esc key. Once the mouse pointer goes back to normal, you're safe—but while the bar is active, any menu item you click will disappear. You can use Tools, Customize to put the victim back—or to restore all the defaults if you can't keep track of what you've lost—but it's much better not to shoot holes in your own menus in the first place.

So how does the little devil get turned on? Just press Ctrl+Alt+[hyphen] and there it is. (Ctrl+Alt+[equal sign] starts a corresponding add-item tool on many but not all systems; also not helpful to anyone who isn't building a complex template, but not nearly so dangerous.) I've left the two shortcuts alone on my computer so I can refresh my memory about how they work, but it might be a good idea to reassign them to a macro that does nothing at all instead (there's one in Chapter 8). Do not assign these keys to something useful unless you're sure you'll never, ever be working on someone else's (unreconstructed) copy of Word!

Update: The destruction tool turns out to have one safe (or at least essential) use: it's the only way to remove a file from the Work menu (described in Chapter 4) without pushing it off the bottom. Tools, Customize won't touch the list of files. So if you put something on the Work menu for a short-term project and want to replace it without adding so many files it drops to #10 and so off the list, Ctrl+Alt+[hyphen] is the tool to use. Carefully.

WHY WORD CAN'T REVEAL CODES

Word was born under a hostile star. It entered a market where another product—WordPerfect—was the clear master, and many of the design decisions that make up its core seem to have had "not how WP does it" as a primary criterion.

Some of these decisions just don't matter. For example, it's hardly significant to talk about "Find" instead of "Search" or to use a keyboard hot key for the tool instead of a function key to get a different and thus marketable "look and feel."

And some reflect a reasonable quest for a new slice of the market. WP provided brilliant support for people who expected to learn how to get something done and then go do it for themselves, using the software as a tool kit. So Word's developers turned it into a sort of secretary-in-a-box, attempting to deduce what its users wanted to do and then help them do it without requiring any knowledge on their part. That's where the Office Assistants—inane Clippy and its cousins—enter the picture, along with the many aggressively helpful default settings we've been pruning.

But some of the decisions are dreadful. When something splits neatly into "good" and "bad," the first-comer has selected "good," and the new guy refuses to duplicate a choice, what's left isn't pretty. To my mind, the greatest of these bloopers is the architecture of the files. (Of course, I wasn't present at any of the deliberations, and I'm sure Microsoft could come up with a dozen reasons why its way is better—but it'd be hard to persuade me that they don't have a strong whiff of fox to them: Aesop's fox, the one who gnawed off his own tail to get out of a trap and then spent the rest of his life trying to persuade all the other foxes how much better life was without that great hairy lump dangling behind.)

To WordPerfect, a file is a simple sequential ribbon of bits and bytes. One follows another without regard to what kind of thing it is. If you had a file consisting of one sentence, say, "This is a *good* idea!" centered on the first line and then repeated on the next line at the left margin, WP would see it (and present it to a user who pressed the function key for Reveal Codes) as something like this:

```
[Open Style: DocumentStyle;][Just: Center]This◊is◊a◊[ItalicOn]
good[ItalicOff]◊idea![HardReturn][Just: Left]This◊is◊a◊
[ItalicOn]good[ItalicOff]◊idea![HardReturn]
```

The stuff in square brackets represents codes embedded in the text stream, which otherwise consists of letters, spaces (shown as little lozenges), and punctuation marks. When a code turns something on, that function stays on until something else overrides it or turns it off. You can search on specific codes as though they were text—for example, to find trailing or leading spaces incorrectly placed inside rather than outside italics. You can also double-click a code and bring up a dialog that lets you modify it.

Word, by contrast, splits up the contents of the document into different units. That is, it stores the text stream in one unit. Then it stores the information about the way each paragraph and the characters in it look (style, alignment on the margin, presence or absence of italics or other special effects at specific points) in another part of the file—off in another direction, as it were—which it represents on the screen as the pilcrow that ends the paragraph. That means anything you do to a paragraph stays in that paragraph, and you have to select the whole region of the file that you want to change if you want to work on more than one paragraph at a time. In the mysterious space indicated by the last pilcrow of the file, it stores information about the file as a whole. If the file has section breaks, the last pilcrow in a section carries whatever specialized info Word needs about that section. Unlike Reveal Codes, this system offers no way to use print to represent what's really happening, but I think of it as a sort of reverse-

Aesop deal: Instead of getting rid of one great hairy lump dangling behind, this fox stuck a bunch of them all over his mangy hide.

So the answer to the eternal question of every WP user forced into Word— "Why can't the lying bastards just show me the blasted codes?"—really is "They can't." The clear and elegant WP code stream has been butchered into segments full of pointers to one another, and no force on earth can change it back.

Word 2002+ makes a spirited attempt to fill the gap with what it calls the "Reveal Formatting" pane, which opens on the right side of the screen and lists everything Word knows about the paragraph you're in or a block of text you select. This can help you spot problems—but most of the time, especially if you're working primarily with semantic content and not with appearance, the easiest way to deal with something that looks funny is to kill all the formatting and reapply what it's supposed to have:

- To get rid of character-level formatting such as italics, select the offending text and press Ctrl+[space]. That restores the text to the basic provisions of the style attached to the paragraph.
- To get rid of the paragraph style, press Ctrl+Shift+N. That almost always reassigns the Normal style, eliminating any paragraph-level style that may have been applied.
- If a style refuses to convert to Normal—and for some reason, "Normal (Web)" is a big offender, but it's not alone—go to the Style dialog and delete the style you want to get rid of. Once it's gone, the text will revert to Normal.

There's also a product on the market called CrossEyes that serves as a Reveal Codes add-in for Word and comes remarkably close to the real thing. (See Chapter 7 for more on this.)

"Help" for WordPerfect Users

Here's where the war gets *nasty*. Some of the little boxes on Tools, Options offer to set things up so as to make life easier for people who are coming in from WordPerfect, but as far as I can tell they're really designed to persuade adventurous Word users that they'd better not stray off the reservation. The WP emulation they set up is an attempt at WP 5.1 for DOS. Perfect though that program may have been in and for its own environment, you don't want anything to do with it in your twenty-first-century Word installation.

The one WP relic that might come in handy is on Tools, Options, Compatibility: "Do full justification like WordPerfect 6.x for Windows." It produces a paragraph with somewhat better spacing than the native Word algorithm can make—but an editor rarely has to worry about justified text, anyway. I leave that sort of thing to the page-makeup folks.

MASTER DOCUMENTS

WordPerfect also had master documents that worked. You could set up a master file, identify things like headers and footers, and designate a whole series of other files that you could deal with either through the master or individually, then print them with one continuous run of page numbers and following all the formatting decisions you made in the master file.

Word doesn't. At any rate, the only person I ever heard claim to make master documents behave reliably was a Word guru of such arcane sapience that I couldn't understand half his answers in the discussion forums where he posted. The universal and easily understood advice from other sources: Don't touch master docs in Word.

This of course makes printing out a book with many chapters in separate files a true pain. To get the pagination to run smoothly without combining the files into one huge and fragile unit, you have to set each chapter to start on the page after the one where its predecessor really ends—and that is a fugitive value that can change depending on the exact printer assigned to the job. The controls are at Insert, Page Numbers, Format, in case you wind up with a client who doesn't take over that part of the job.

AUTOMATIC NUMBERING

I never made enough use of WordPerfect's automatic list function to know if Word went wrong in another attempt to get away from a right answer ... but wrong it went. Automated lists in Word sort of work, which puts them ahead of master docs, but they're finicky and temperamental, and everyone agrees they've been broken from the get-go and are broken still.

When they work, the automated lists are enormously helpful, so authors like them a lot. Much better than trying to remember to keep the numbers straight by hand, particularly while you're adding, deleting, and shuffling items on a list! And if a list is the only one in a file, it probably won't misbehave.

Unfortunately, multiple lists tend to get on each other's nerves, sometimes to the point of making Word refuse to restart the numbering when told to do so or otherwise lose track of how they're supposed to look. When that happens, it's not anything you did wrong, and there's no one way out of the hole; just fiddle with the file until you get something you can use. In a pinch, you can switch from the regular automatic numbers to field codes, which work much more reliably. You can find instructions at www.knopf.com/tips/autonumber.html. (I'm told that you can ignore the references to RoboHelp; the solution is said to work just fine in Word itself.)

People who really need numbering to work—law firms and the like—invariably buy an after-market product to take care of it for them. Most publishers want the numbers converted to regular text during the edit, so editors can get along with a simpler tool. There's a very basic converter in the archive mentioned in "More Help with Macros" in Chapter 4, and the Editorium (discussed in Chapter 7) has one called "ListFixer" that I've often seen recommended, though I stick with my own version.

FIELDS AT PLAY

As noted, one way authors get around the problem with automated lists is to use field codes: snippets that translate to different values of text depending on internal or external conditions, and are good for lots of things in addition to lists. Field codes are not broken; they work quite nicely—but not for publishers, as they invariably make the page-makeup stage of production cough up its guts. So all a publisher's editor needs to know about fields is how to recognize them and how to get rid of them.

Hyperlinks behave like fields in many ways (and you can kill them along with the rest of the fields), but they're not quite the same beast. The main pitfall they offer is their persistence; several apparently logical countermeasures just conceal them without actually cutting them. I heard of one document where the author had put in a dummy—but active—hyperlink full of *x*'s to indicate that it was a fake. The text was later deleted, but the spot in the file stayed live ... and curious readers clicking the little hand that mysteriously appeared there were taken straight to a porn site.

Recognizing Fields

- On Tools, Options, View, set "Field Shading" to "Always." That will turn the background of the screen a different color behind a field, so you can tell what you're dealing with.
- On Tools, Customize, Commands, drag View, View Field Codes up to a toolbar. That will let you toggle fields between their calculated values and their formulas, which can be very useful if your author has employed EndNote or some other add-in that uses fields to accomplish something in the files.

You don't need to do anything about hyperlinks to make them visible; they show up as blue underlined text if you haven't changed the default.

Killing Fields

- *To remove one field at a time:* Select the field and press Ctrl+Shift+F9.
- *To remove all the fields from a file at one stroke:* Press Ctrl+A to select all the text, then press Ctrl+Shift+F9. (This won't touch the headers and footers, where page numbers are generally set in fields. You can usually ignore fields in headers and footers, as those parts of the file don't affect page makeup. Unfortunately, this method won't touch embedded endnotes either; to get rid of fields there, you need to select the embedded notes separately.)
- *To remove a hyperlink and replace it with its text:* Move the insertion point into the linked text, then press Ctrl+K to get to the Insert Hyperlink dialog and Alt+R to break the link.
- *To make sure you don't inadvertently insert new links:* Go to Tools, Auto-Correct Options, AutoFormat As You Type and make sure the box for replacing Internet and network paths with hyperlinks is not checked.

UNDEAD TEXT

So you're editing along, Track Changes active but out of sight, and you select and type over an ill-chosen word. Unbeknownst to you, the formerly adjacent word, already deleted and now hidden in the tracking, reappears on the screen behind where you're working, just as though you'd typed it in again on purpose. You, of course, looking where you're going and not where you've been, see nothing, and later wonder how you could have been such a doofus.

This eerie resurrection of text happened a lot in Word 97. Today as I write in Word 2003, I can't get it to show up ... but I'm sure I've seen it on the new system. The word "you're" seems to have an especially strong grip on the afterlife. Not a whole lot you can do about this; it's a real-for-real crawling bug. Just be aware of the possibility, and if you think you see it, well, it's not you that's buggy.

CHAR CHAR CHAR

Word 2002+ has a whole new trick. If you select part of a paragraph and assign a paragraph style to it (rather than a character style), Word decides that you wanted to create a whole new character style with the same font attributes as the paragraph style. Word names it "[paragraphstylename] Char" to make the connection clear. Do it again, and you get "[paragraphstylename] Char Char"—and so on.

So what's wrong with that? Well, it clutters up the list of styles something awful, but the real kicker is that if you delete one of the "Char" styles, Word happily deletes the underlying paragraph style, too. This happens because the character and paragraph styles are linked; changes to one automatically propagate to the other.

Because these linked styles are so confusing, Microsoft issued a patch that hides them so they don't show up in the Styles listing if your copy of Word 2002 is up to date or you're using Word 2003. But they're still there if you've made any—you can see them at Tools, Templates and Add-ins, Organizer, and anyone can see them if the document is opened in Word 97 or Word 2000.

The best thing to do, as ever, is not get into this hole in the first place. Here's how:

- Never select any text when applying a paragraph style to a single paragraph. (Multiple paragraphs are no problem because a paragraph mark is always included in the selection, so Word doesn't leap to unwarranted conclusions about your intent to create a new style.)
- Apply only character styles to selected text.

But if it's too late and the problem already exists, Cindy Meister, a Microsoft MVP, has a macro on her website—at www.homepage.swissonline.ch/cindymeister/MyFavTip.htm#CharStyl—that may help fix the problem.

7 LOCATING USEFUL ADDITIONS

With so much available within Word, you need more? Yup. Not *need*, per-haps—but there's a lot out there that will make your editing even faster and more congenial than it is with everything introduced thus far.

EDITORIUM PRODUCTS

Jack Lyon of the Editorium (www.editorium.com) is a working editor with a taste for Word, and he's produced a wide range of add-ins that really add. His Editor's Toolkit Plus product is probably the equivalent of three years' intensive experience and experimentation with customizing your system to make it fly—plus several tools that are well beyond most do-it-yourself macro programmers.

If you're just starting out and your copy of Word is pretty much plain va-nilla, give Editor's Toolkit Plus a try—free for forty-five days, then less than a hundred bucks to keep; a week of playing with it should put you ahead of a class that costs several times as much and runs half a year. And take a look at the Freebies page of the site, too.

It's a grief to me that I had about five years' intensive customization in my system when I first discovered the Editorium, so it felt like too much mental retreading to rearrange my reflexes to yet another new keyboard. What I've done instead is pick up several of his stand-alone tools:

- *FileCleaner:* Offers an array of choices for getting rid of typewriter-brained errors in edit files—including bad spacing and lowercase *l* instead of nu-meral 1—that (like all of Jack's stuff) you can apply to a single file, a set of open files, or all the files in a directory.
- *MegaReplacer:* Takes your list of find-and-replace decisions (regarding text, character formatting, or styles) and applies them to the usual array of files. You can choose whether or not to track the results, and whether to let the routine run by itself or stop and ask you about each decision. You can also save the list for future use—or delete it once you're done with it. This is the product mentioned in Chapter 1 as a way to wipe out global errors in a manuscript.
- *MultiMacro:* Applies your list of macros in the order you specify. The protection-for-tracked-changes macros in Chapter 8 rely on this

add-in for effortless and complete application to a whole book's worth of files.

- *NoteStripper:* Converts footnotes and endnotes from Word's embedded facility to plain text—and vice versa, so they renumber themselves. Pays for itself the first time an author decides to delete note 3 and note 68 of 175 and scatter a few new notes through the chapter at the last minute.

- *Puller:* Gives you a list of delimited items—things in parentheses, straight or angle brackets, or other codes you specify—which is especially useful for checking up on your typemarking. You can see every single one you used, identified by file, or get a consolidated list stripped of duplicates.

- *RazzmaTag:* Converts Word formatting to user codes and vice versa. It's designed for tagging files for QuarkXPress and other typesetting programs, so I make little use of it—but it's handy when it's handy—if only for its ability to generate a bunch of files in plain text instead of Word format.

- *WordCounter:* Gives you a table of word, character, and both Word-generated page counts and counts calculated based on 250-word pages for the usual array of files; essential for figuring project rates. (It will also give you a concordance of a file, with or without indicating how many times a word was used.)

These are all tools, not wizards, so they take some practice to use effectively. But they all come with detailed manuals and help screens—and if you run into trouble, you can always write to Jack and get an answer (or a fix, if you've found a new problem).

OTHER SUPPORT PROGRAMS
Jack's not the only game in town. A working editor should also have a variety of software besides Word to help get the job done. Books could be (and have been) written about every one of these issues; this is the merest sketch of the kinds of things to think about.

Basic Security   ✈ *1.a*
It's a bad old world out there. When your livelihood depends on your computer, protect it—against viruses, spyware, and other invaders. At the moment, I'm using the free ZoneAlarm firewall (www.zonelabs.com), F-Prot antivirus software (www.f-prot.com), and both Spybot Search and Destroy (www.safer-networking.org) and Ad-Aware (www.lavasoftusa.com) for antispyware—

in addition to staying away from Internet Explorer as much as possible (and Outlook entirely; I use Firefox and Thunderbird) and using an ISP (Earthlink) that's pretty good at keeping the do-bads at bay. I also subscribe to Brian Livingston's *Windows Secrets* newsletter (www.windowssecrets.com) to stay current with Microsoft's adventures, though I don't always follow his advice.

File Conversion

Back in the day—before Word ate the market—an editor couldn't live without a really good converter to translate files from one program's layout to another's. I still keep a utility called Conversions Plus (from www.dataviz.com) on my system, but it's been several years since I've used it.

File Transfer

These days most jobs involve e-mailing files back and forth, but for very large files or relatively slow connections, you'll probably find e-mail inconvenient. At that point you'll want a file transfer protocol (FTP) manager, which will allow you to hook up to a website directly and download or upload your files. I use FTP Explorer (from www.ftpx.com), an inexpensive and easy-to-use program that allows drag-and-drop file transfers, background downloading, and other useful features.

Backup

Computers get more and more reliable every year, but there's still truth in this sad maxim:

> A hard drive that has never crashed
> is a hard drive that hasn't crashed yet.

And even short of a drive crash, any number of things can come between you and the files that earn you your living. I use Acronis True Image 11 (www. acronis.com) to make a compressed backup of my whole hard drive every week, copying to a dismountable second drive after clearing the temp files and Recycle Bin. Then, each evening, I copy the day's updated working files to a CD using a program called Backup Magic (www.moonsoftware.com). The Acronis is a recent upgrade that now does incremental backups—which its predecessor did not—but I haven't explored that yet, largely because the external drive is a nuisance to load and unload.

Optical Character Recognition

A scanner is such a good toy, it's pleasant that it's business-related. The more often part of a job comes in on paper, of course, the more useful a scanner is, but eventually almost any editor will find it handy to be able to suck words off paper without using the eye-hand input process. Even if your scanner comes with some sort of optical character recognition (OCR) software, as most do, it's a good idea to take a look at the top of the line. I'm using OmniPage Pro (www. omnipage.com) now, but I've heard rumors that it's been surpassed. ABBYY FineReader (www.abbyy.com) comes well recommended.

Dictionary

If you're working in a specialized field, you may be able to buy a dictionary add-in that will augment Word's spelling checker with the terminology of the field. Ask on one of the editors' mailing lists, and your remote colleagues will advise. In addition, regular dictionaries (such as *Merriam-Webster's Collegiate Dictionary*, 11th edition) now come with CDs that you can run instead of picking up the book to look something up. I still use the paper version, however, because it makes a good break to call on my big arm muscles instead of the finger-twiddling variety.

Reveal Codes

CrossEyes from Levit and James opens a panel very similar to WordPerfect's Reveal Codes—but goes WP one better, as it will hide all the text except that adjacent to changes in formatting. I was reluctant even to try this product for years, as I'd found ways to live without Reveal Codes and figured the best CrossEyes could do would be a translation, subject to error of its own. But a demonstration was impressive, and if I had to deal with the details of formatting, I think I'd find it worthwhile. You can read more about it and download a trial copy at www.levitjames.com/crosseyes/reveal-the-codes. htm.

Compression Managers

If double-clicking a *zip file* name doesn't make it open, Windows users should go to www.winzip.com and download the current version of WinZip. Mac users probably want Stuffit from Aladdin Systems (www.stuffit.com). These programs aren't free, but they have trial periods—and something along these lines is an indispensable part of modern computing.

BOOKS AND RESOURCES
Word is a living exemplar of my father's favorite maxim:

It's supposed to be easy.
If it's not easy, you're doing it wrong.

He was referring to tools and mechanical things, but it holds true for software. Whatever you have to do in Word should be nearly effortless—and if you don't know how to make it effortless, you need more information. And even if it already seems pretty well effortless, you still can use more information—much of what I know about Word's byways comes from a habit of subscribing to any source of free and reasonably reliable info that crosses my path. Here are some places to turn when just asking Word, via the sometimes useful Help system, doesn't get you what you need:

- Jack Lyon, *Microsoft Word for Publishing Professionals.* Softcover book that basically consists of several years' accumulation from Jack's newsletter, *Editorium Update,* along with other articles and things he's written—600+ pages of tips, tricks, and macros. It's available at the Editorium site, www. editorium.com. (You can subscribe to the newsletter, which is free, and search the newsletter archives there, too.)
- Geoff Hart, *Effective Onscreen Editing: New Tools for an Old Profession.* The big book on on-screen editing—my pdf copy runs 723 pages. It's full of general advice on the business of editing, plus how to use any word processor to make your life easier, with specific techniques illustrated using Word as an example. To order, visit Geoff's Web site (www.geoff-hart. com). While you're at the site, have a look at Geoff's Resources page (www.geoff-hart.com/resources.html)—lots of useful info there, including the full text of many of his articles on technical writing, editing, information design, backup and security, and even avoiding repetitive stress injuries, linked from the bibliography item at the top of the page.
- Allen Wyatt, *WordTips.* Free e-mail newsletter from www.vitalnews.com, which also has a number of inexpensive and useful collections of hints and tools.
- Word-PC. Free e-mail discussion group for users of Word on PC equipment—good for heavy-duty advice and macro programming tips. To join, send a blank e-mail message to word-pc-subscribe-request@liverpool.ac.uk; "blank" means no text, no sig line, nothing.

- McEdit. Yahoo discussion group for users of Word on Mac equipment; I'm monoglot PC myself and have no direct experience with this list, but people speak well of it. To join, send a blank e-mail message to McEdit-subscribe@yahoogroups.com.

- Electric Editors (www.electriceditors.net). Based in England, this site offers discussion groups and an interesting collection of free Word macros. (And WordPerfect macros as well, if you ever need to cross the Great Divide.)

- Cindy Meister. The Word MVP quoted earlier in these pages has lots of interesting stuff on her website: www.homepage.swissonline.ch/cindy-meister/index.html.

- Shauna Kelly, another online Word wiz. Her site (aptly called "Making the Most of Word in Your Business") provides clear and cogent answers, starting with a page that works even if you're not sure of the question: www.shaunakelly.com/word/index.html.

8 A BOUQUET OF SAMPLE SHORTCUTS

My first and most important shortcut set isn't here. It's a package of four macros—originally written for WordPerfect for DOS and later redone for WordPerfect for Windows and again for MS Word—that make it possible to consolidate a book's worth of chapter-level bibliographies in one file, sort them together, pull out the parts of references that identify edited collections so they can be dealt with as a separate group for consistency, restore them to their original reference entries, deal with all the various errors chapter authors have made in the references as a whole, and then restore all the references, in their proper order, to the chapters they came from. The set is too temperamental for general release, but it works—I've used it successfully on manuscripts whose chapters collectively carried upwards of a thousand reference items.

I mention it here only because it marks a defining moment in my onscreen editing career. On my very first commercial electronic edit, I spent twelve hours on the bibliographies for a journal whose time budget—the amount of time I could afford to spend and still make the lowest effective rate I felt good about accepting—was twenty hours. (No, I didn't finish within my time budget on that one!) It was painfully clear that I faced a choice—either I had to tell the client I wouldn't do that sort of job again, or I had to find a better way.

On screen, there's always a better way. This chapter provides a few to get you started. One way to use them is to copy the text from "Sub" through "End Sub" and then click Tools, Macro, Macros; type the macro name; click Create; paste the text over the lines that say "Sub [macroname()]" and "End Sub" in the resulting screen; and close out the screen. (Note that any line that begins with a single quote mark is for you to read so you can understand what the next lines do; your computer will ignore it.) For more detailed instructions, work through the exercises suggested under "More Help with Macros" in Chapter 4.

SERIAL COMMA

One of the many fracture points in U.S. society seems to lie between people who publish books and those who write them—the former insisting on the serial comma and the latter almost universally eschewing it. As a result, many edits have scarcely a paragraph that doesn't demand the addition of a comma somewhere—sometimes more than once in a sentence. With the following macro in

Normal.dot and bound to a hot key, you can create the comma where it belongs from wherever you notice the need, rather than mousing to the spot itself. (Especially if you make another copy of the macro, replacing "and" with "or," and put it on an adjacent hot key.)

```
Sub SerialAnd()
' Macro written 02/27/03 by Hilary Powers
   Selection.Find.ClearFormatting
   With Selection.Find
      .text = "and"
      .MatchCase = True
      .MatchWholeWord = True
   End With
   Selection.Find.Execute
   Selection.MoveLeft Unit:=wdCharacter, Count:=2
   Selection.TypeText text:=","
   Selection.MoveRight Unit:=wdWord, Count:=2
End Sub
```

ADDING *ING*

In the course of smoothing out a sentence, it's often useful to change a present-tense or past-tense verb into a gerund, but selecting the unneeded characters and typing in *ing* rapidly gets old. With this macro on a hot key, all you have to do is put the insertion point where you want the *i* and turn it loose.

```
Sub IngyDingy()
' Macro recorded 10/22/05 by Hilary Powers
   Selection.MoveRight Unit:=wdWord, Count:=1, Extend:=wdExtend
   Selection.TypeText text:="ing"
End Sub
```

CITATION CHECKING

As promised in Chapter 1, the first of the following macros allows you to select a whole citation or group of citations with one hot key—after you put the insertion point at the beginning, which may be inside or outside the parens with the date. The second picks up the selected text, copies it to the other open document, advances to a new line there, and then returns to the main document and moves just to the right of the next opening paren.

```
Sub Fillerup()
' Macro cannibalized by Hilary Powers 1/30/04
Selection.Extend
Selection.Extend Character:=")"
End Sub
```

```
Sub GetThat()
' Macro recorded 1/29/04 by Hilary Powers; Window-switching
' line (which won't record properly in Word 2003) refixed
' per Jack Lyon of the Editorium, 1/30/04
Selection.Copy
WordBasic.NextWindow
Selection.PasteAndFormat (wdPasteDefault)
Selection.TypeParagraph
WordBasic.NextWindow
Selection.MoveRight Unit:=wdCharacter, Count:=1
Selection.Find.ClearFormatting
With Selection.Find
.text = "("
.Forward = True
.Wrap = wdFindContinue
End With
Selection.Find.Execute
Selection.MoveRight Unit:=wdCharacter, Count:=1
End Sub
```

Do Nothing

If you wind up with a hot key—the one that activates the Magic Menu Destruction tool, for example—that you're sure you don't want, you can take it out of play by assigning this macro to it. (Much safer than putting something you do want to do there, as that risks trouble if you're ever on someone else's system.)

```
Sub DoNothing()
' I'm empty
End Sub
```

 1.b

STYLE SHEET MAINTENANCE

One of the joys of electronic editing is the ease of preparing a style sheet, but the cut-and-paste sequence can still get tiresome after a while. In the following macros, the first copies selected text and places it on the style sheet (the second of the two documents you have open for this trick), then stops there so you can add the part of speech or otherwise adjust the pasted text. The second puts a blank line in the style sheet and moves to it, returns to the main document, and clears the selection.

```
Sub StyleThat()
' Macro adapted from GetThat by Hilary Powers 1/30/04
Selection.Copy
WordBasic.NextWindow
Selection.PasteAndFormat (wdPasteDefault)
End Sub


Sub HedOnBack()
' Macro adapted from GetThat by Hilary Powers 1/30/04
Selection.TypeParagraph
WordBasic.NextWindow
Selection.MoveRight Unit:=wdCharacter, Count:=1
End Sub
```

CLEAR TRACKING FROM FORMAT CHANGES

Word 2002+ will insist on tracking changes in formatting if you're tracking anything at all, which makes clearing the tracking after author review much more difficult. If you want to get all the formatting out of play at once, the following macro will do the job. (This is one of my favorite toys, created after years of intermittent nibbling at the problem. I keep it on Alt+Ctrl+Shift+F.)

```
Sub AcceptFormatChanges()
' Macro cobbled up 8/14/06 by Hilary Powers
' Based on commands revealed by Keri Morgret
' Use only on file that opens with all markup visible!
' Next four lines toggle all display of changes off.
   WordBasic.ShowFormatting
   WordBasic.ShowInkAnnotations
```

```
   WordBasic.ShowInsertionsAndDeletions
   WordBasic.ShowComments
' Toggle display of formatting back on.
   WordBasic.ShowFormatting
' Approve formatting changes.
   WordBasic.AcceptAllChangesShown
' Next three lines toggle everything else back on.
   WordBasic.ShowInsertionsAndDeletions
   WordBasic.ShowComments
   WordBasic.ShowInkAnnotations
End Sub
```

PROTECTING FOR TRACKED CHANGES

Here are the macros promised in Chapter 5 for setting and removing protection for tracked changes. You can run them on one file at a time, but they work best when combined with the Editorium's MultiMacro product. Paste your own choice in between the quotes where they say "mypassword," which I assure you is not what I use.

```
Sub TrackPassword()
' Macro recorded 05/05/03 by Hilary Powers
   ActiveDocument.TrackRevisions = Not ActiveDocument.
      TrackRevisions
   ActiveDocument.Protect Password:="mypassword",
      NoReset:=False, Type:=wdAllowOnlyRevisions
End Sub
```

```
Sub TrackRemPswd()
' Macro written 05/05/03 by Hilary Powers
If ActiveDocument.ProtectionType = wdNoProtection Then GoTo Last
   ActiveDocument.Unprotect Password:="mypassword"
Last:
End Sub
```

FIXING THE DOCUMENT MAP

As I said in Chapter 2, the Document Map is the best way to stay oriented in a long file. Unfortunately, it sometimes loses its bearings and starts putting all sorts of short paragraphs into the list, making it essentially unusable. This macro will fix it when that happens, as long as you're using the built-in heading styles and not user styles to which you've assigned heading levels. It won't stick when you close the file—the next time you look, the Document Map will be back to its old tricks—but it's easy enough to run the macro again and get something you can work with.

```
Sub BodyText()
' Macro written 10/28/99 by Shawn Vincent Wilson
' Changes all paragraph outline levels to Body Text, clearing
' unwanted lines out of Document Map. The built-in heading styles
' are for some reason immune to the change, so there's no special
' code to retain their levels.
' Forwarded with permission, as long as author's name stays attached.
For Each aGraf In ActiveDocument.Paragraphs
    aGraf.Style.AutomaticallyUpdate = False
    If aGraf.OutlineLevel <> wdOutlineLevelBodyText Then _
        aGraf.OutlineLevel = wdOutlineLevelBodyText
Next aGraf
End Sub
```

FINDING MORE WITHOUT ASKING FOR IT

As noted in Chapter 4, Microsoft's insistence on opening a short version of the Find and Replace dialog really bugs me—the long dialog has no disadvantages, and hiding it is just more "don't bother your pretty little head, dear." With this macro in the Startup folder, Word opens and expands the dialog for you ... most of the time. For some reason, it doesn't always work, but it feels like about 95% on my machine.

```
Sub AutoExec()
' Written by David Chinnell, May 2008
Application.ScreenUpdating = False
SendKeys "%(M)"
Dialogs(wdDialogEditReplace).Display TimeOut:=1000
Application.ScreenUpdating = True
End Sub
```

9 WALKING THROUGH A JOB

Every edit is different ... but they tend to follow a pattern, with certain kinds of chores most useful at certain times. Here is a rough outline of what I'd expect to do on almost any manuscript:

1. Set up the job.
    a. Get the files—probably by e-mail these days, or downloaded from the client's FTP site.
    b. Run your virus checker before opening anything—or even moving the files out of the download directory.
    c. Set up a directory for the project—with, at minimum, a subdirectory for the untouched original files. (I keep the working files in the main project directory, where they're easy to get at.)
    d. Look over the hard copy (if there is any; it's nice but not essential to have it), and transfer any notes from the client to the files.
    e. Start the style sheet. I keep a master sheet for each client with the essentials of that client's requirements already filled in, and make a copy of it for each job. (See Figure 3.)
2. Do a preliminary cleanup.
    a. Run a mechanical setup macro to work around the author's typewriter-use habits. (Jack Lyon's FileCleaner is good if the client doesn't specify a setup set.)
    b. Turn on Track Changes.
    c. Do generic fixes via MegaReplacer, telling it to track the results. (My global-replace file includes things like changing *advisor* to *adviser* and *email* to *e-mail*—so as to fix stuff authors almost universally do and publishers equally universally avoid. The tracking makes it easy to undo any changes to titles and quotes, which need to stand as-was.)
    d. Load or attach any client-specific or editing-environment templates.
3. Edit the references so that each entry in the file follows the style laid down for the book. Doing this up front primes my brain with the vocabulary of the job and gives me a feel for how carefully the author has worked.

4. Consolidate the text citations, as described in Chapter 1. I do this chapter by chapter, before the detailed edit, not all at once.

5. Make the first edit pass. That is, read word by word and do whatever the assignment requires as it appears.

   a. Copy and paste terms reflecting decisions on usage, hyphenation, and whatnot to the style sheet.

   b. Fix characteristic errors globally.

   c. Fact-check anything that feels twitchy. (The Internet is your friend here. For a more tailored search than Google allows, try Clusty at www.clusty.com.)

   d. Enter queries in the form the client prefers—Inline, Comment, Footnote—remembering that there's plenty of room to be polite and attentive to the author's nerves, and that abbreviations and cryptic notes are best avoided entirely. (I use AutoCorrect or AutoText for things I ask or explain often.)

   e. Edit the figures on hard copy (if required); if not, insert notes describing any necessary changes in the text—either where the figure is first cited, in the figure caption, or in the art file. Check the art to be sure it supports the text and contains no contradictions to the text.

   f. Typemark headings, text, and other markup features as required. Macros are very useful for this step.

6. Vet the list of citations against the references and query as needed.

7. Check the table of contents against chapter titles and query as needed.

8. Typemark the file openers. I like to do this in one sitting, as the book-title running head is provided by a macro that gets updated from project to project.

9. Make the second edit pass. Read everything again and fix whatever needs fixing.

   a. Be alert for verbatim repetition. (For some reason, I rarely notice this on the first reading, but the second time through, a phrase will strike a chord—at which point a file search often reveals that the author has said something the same way twice—or more.)

   b. Check the revision marks to be sure they make sense.

10. Clean up the files.

   a. Convert the footnotes or endnotes from the embedded Word feature if necessary. (But it's often better to leave them alone until after the author reviews the manuscript.)

   b. Review the queries for sense and tone.

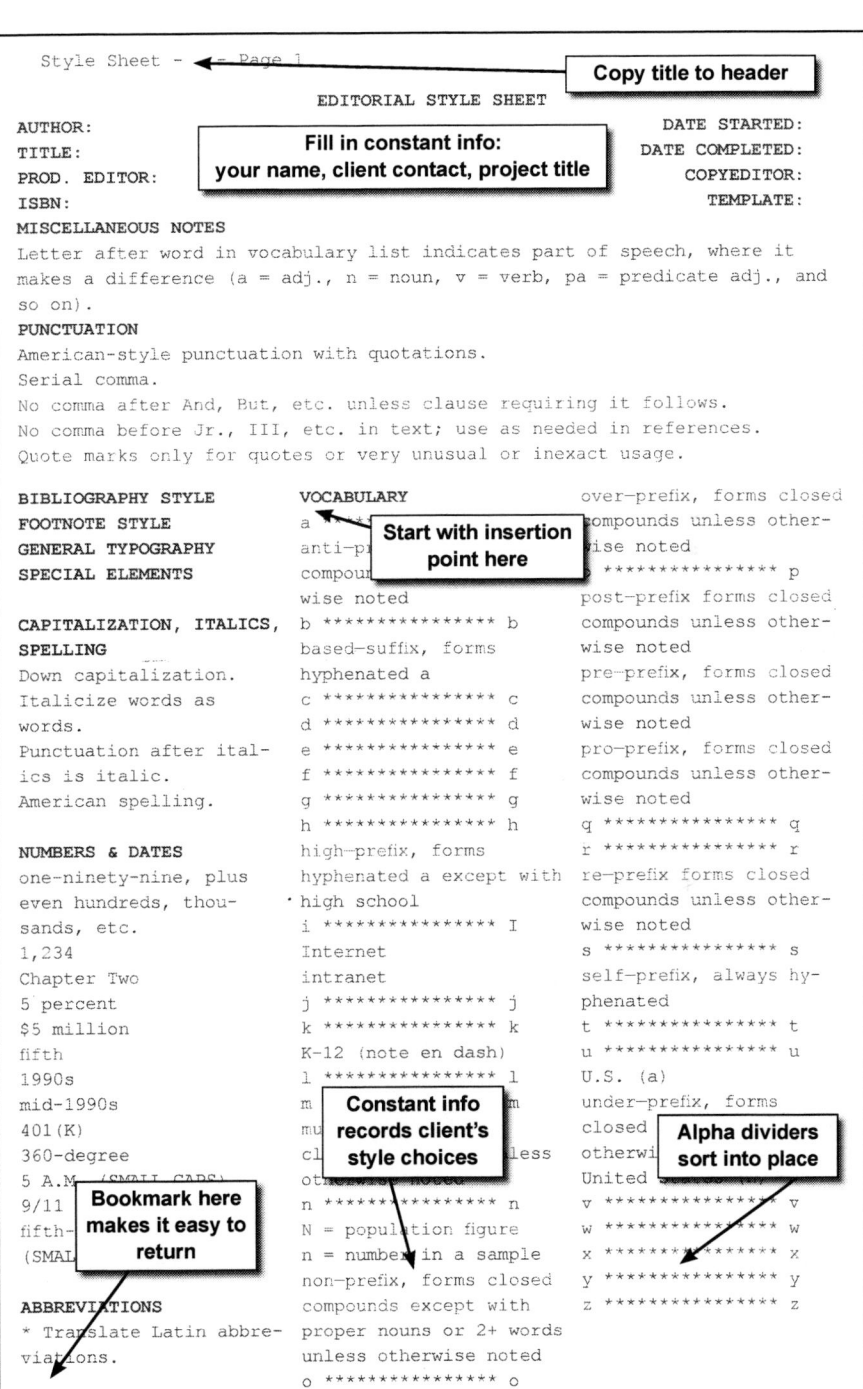

Figure 3. Sample Style Sheet Master

    c.   Check the spelling—with a dictionary at hand!

    d.   Add new words from the spelling check to the style sheet.

11. Finish the style sheet.

    a.   Sort each section and remove duplicate entries.

    b.   Check out any conflicts and correct the files as needed.

    c.   Add the completion date.

12. Prepare the cover letter and invoice, close up the job, and send it off.

This process assumes that the files will return to me after the author reviews them, and I will then resolve the queries and clear the tracking. If I'm not going to see the files again, in step 10 I will also check the typemarking and make sure italics and boldface are applied to adjacent punctuation and spaces (or left off them) as the client requires.

Oh—and one more step: Calculate the pages-per-hour throughput on the job and the effective hourly rate it paid, and spend a few minutes thinking about what happened and what could have been further automated so as to go faster with the same or improved quality. On screen, there's always a better way. ...

INDEX

ABOUT THE AUTHOR

Hilary Powers has been freelancing since mid-1994, when she settled on editing as the skill most likely to allow her to emulate Nero Wolfe and avoid leaving home on business. She started working on screen before the end of that year, and abandoned paper entirely after only four projects. Now, somewhere north of 475 projects later, she still learns some new trick or shortcut on almost every job.

Editing is her fourth career. She's settled into it happily for the long term, after working as a government analyst, an internal auditor and computer security specialist, and a nonprofit manager. For more info, see her Web site at www.powersedit.com.

Other EFA Publications and Resources

The EFA has a variety of resources available on topics of interest to editorial freelancers.

Books and booklets published by the EFA cover subjects such as electronic editing, résumé preparation, grammar, copyright and permissions, book production, textbook development, and organizing a freelance business. For a current list and ordering information, visit www.the-efa.org/res/booklets.php.

The EFA website, www.the-efa.org, offers a number of online resources. Popular are the "Code of Fair Practice," which defines ethical standards and contract guidelines for editorial freelancers and clients; a table of "Common Rates for Editorial Services"; a list of online reference sources such as specialized websites and dictionaries; and an archive of articles from *The Freelance Editorial Association News*, the official publication of the now-defunct FEA.

The EFA newsletter, *The Freelancer,* features articles on freelance and communications issues, book and software reviews, columns on taxes and language usage, reports on EFA meetings and activities, letters from readers, and more. Published bimonthly, it is a complimentary benefit of EFA membership. Nonmembers pay a low $20 for an annual subscription.